Property of Arkansas Library Commission
Little Rock, Arkansas

The Works of Philip Freneau: A Critical Study

by

Philip M. Marsh

The Scarecrow Press, Inc.
Metuchen, N.J. 1968

L. C. Card No. 68-12620

Contents

Page

Preface v

Chronology 7

Chapters

1. Introduction 11
   - I Freneau's Fame
   - II Biography

2. The College Poet 20
   - I Pre-College Background
   - II Undergraduate Poems
   - III A Semi-Epic

3. Other Poems Before 1780 25
   - I Pamphlet Verse of the 1770's
   - II Other Verse of the 1770's
   - III Freneau in the United States Magazine--1779

4. The Poet at His Best, 1780-90 36
   - I Writings in 1780
   - II Poems and Prose, mostly in The Freeman's Journal, 1781-89
   - III The 1786 Poems
   - IV The Miscellaneous Works, 1788

5. The Political Journalist, 1780-1800 56
   - I The 1790 Poems
   - II Essays of 1790
   - III Last Weeks in the Advertiser, 1791
   - IV Poems in the National Gazette
   - V Essays in the National Gazette
   - VI The Almanac and the 1795 Poems
   - VII The Jersey Chronicle and "Tomo Cheeki"
   - VIII The Time Piece, 1797
   - IX Back to Philadelphia
   - X 'Robert Slender II'

6. Looking Back After Victory, 1801-1809 152
   - I Back to Sea
   - II The 1809 Poems

7. The Last Active Years 162
   - I The "Old Soldier" Essays
   - II The 'War of 1812' Years

Page

III The 1815 *Poems*
IV The Post-War Years

8. Critical Conclusions 181

Guide to Notes and References 183

Selected Bibliography 184

Index 189

Preface

The aim of this book is to present a description, an interpretation, and an evaluation of Philip Freneau's poetry and prose. Because he is not widely known outside American literature, a brief life is included; and facts of his character and activities are used to help in establishing his authorship (where it is probable but uncertain), and in some interpretations.

The bulk of Freneau's known poetry is represented in his collected editions, although many of his poems were not included. Most of his prose was never collected; and much of what is assigned to him must be, if at all, by reflections of his personal circumstances, style, pseudonyms, or characteristic ideas.

Because of the large number of poems and essays, it has been necessary to confine this treatment to the more important or characteristic items. The poems here are taken chiefly from his collections of 1786, 1788, 1795, 1809, and 1815; but there were also small pamphlet editions and many poems in newspapers and magazines, not included in his collections. The only collected prose appears in the 1788 _Miscellaneous Works_ and in "Robert Slender's" _Letters_ of 1799. The rest, some thousand essays, must be taken from editorials and newspaper-magazine contributions, both certain and probable.

Libraries consulted were those at Harvard, Yale, Columbia, Rutgers, Princeton, Pennsylvania, and Indiana Universities; at American Antiquarian Society, New York Public Library, New York Historical Society, New Jersey Historical Association, Monmouth County (N. J.) Historical Association, Pennsylvania Historical Society, Ridgway Library (Philadelphia), Library of Congress, Charleston (S. C.) Historical Society, Georgia Historical Society, Huntington Library, and my own collection of Freneau's books.

P. M. M.

Chronology

1752 Born January 2 (old calendar), on Frankfort Street, New York; first child of Pierre Fresneau (old spelling) and Agnes Watson Fresneau.

1767 Pierre Fresneau died, October 17.

1768 Entered, as sophomore, Princeton College (then College of New Jersey), November 7.

1771 Graduated on September 25, with James Madison and Hugh Brackenridge.

1772 Taught thirteen days in Flatbush, Long Island, and left. Published The American Village, with several short poems, in New York.
Published A Poem, on the Rising Glory of America, a collaboration with Brackenridge, in Philadelphia.
Taught at Somerset Academy, Maryland, under Principal Brackenridge.

1773 Probably finished teaching through school year at Somerset Academy.

1774 Studied theology about two years.

1775 Wrote patriotic verse satires on British, in New York, also "The House of Night."
Published American Liberty in New York, also in Philadelphia as The Present Situation of Affairs in North-America.
Published A Voyage to Boston in Philadelphia.

1776 February, sailed from Philadelphia (?) to Santa Cruz, Virgin Islands, guest of Captain John Hanson--and resided with Hanson there over two years.

1777 While living with Hanson, visited islands in the Caribbean; was a member of privateering crews on several ventures.

1778 April, visited Bermuda; courted Frances Bruere, governor's daughter.
July, sailing to the United States, taken by British ship, then released; then he enlisted as private in New Jersey Militia.
About this time, he published American Independence in Philadelphia.

1779 Contributed poems and essays to Brackenridge's United States Magazine, published by Francis Bailey in Philadelphia.
July, master of the John Courter.
September, supercargo on the Rebecca.

1780 Quit the militia on May 1.
May 25, left Philadelphia as passenger on the Aurora, a privateer, and was taken prisoner by a British frigate on May 26.
May 28 to July 13, prisoner in New York Harbor, on ships Scorpion and Hunter.

1781 Published The British Prison Ship, broadside of his capture and imprisonment, accusing British of cruelty, in Philadelphia.
July, began to help edit The Freeman's Journal, Philadelphis, published by Francis Bailey, also contributing poems and essays.

1782 Left Freeman's Journal, August or September.
September (?), began as clerk in Philadelphia post office.

1783 Translated Abbé Robin's New Travels Through North-America, published in Philadelphia--also in Boston, 1784.

1784 June, sailed for Jamaica, as supercargo, on the Dromelly.
July, nearly wrecked in hurricane, near Jamaica.
November, returned to Philadelphia.

1785 January, printing for Patrick Rice, Philadelphia--then left because of illness.
June (?), went to Pacolet Springs, South Carolina, for treatment.
October (?), returned to Monmouth, N. J.
November, sailed as master of the Monmouth, for Charleston, S. C.

1786-1789 Sailed between Philadelphia and New York, to Charleston and Savannah, to West Indian islands, and other ports, as captain of the Monmouth, Industry, and the Columbia.

1786 Bailey in Philadelphia published first full volume of Poems.

1788 Bailey published Freneau's Miscellaneous Works, prose and poetry.

1789 Retired from sea while in Charleston, in November.

1790 Arrived in New York, in February.
March, began to help edit the Daily Advertiser, New York, published by Francis Childs and John Swaine.
April 15, married Eleanor Forman at Middletown Point, N. J. (Matawan), and settled in New York.

1791 January, planned a New Jersey newspaper.
February, Jefferson offered Freneau a part-time translatorship in Department of State, at $250 a year.
March, Freneau declined the offer.
July, agreed to edit newspaper in Philadelphia, with Childs and Swaine as the publishers.
August, accepted the translatorship.
October, published first issue of the National Gazette, Philadelphia.

1792 July, Alexander Hamilton, under pseudonyms in the Gazette of the United States, began attacks on Freneau and Jefferson, charging bribery and collusion, saying Jefferson was the real director of the National Gazette.
August, Freneau denied charges publicly, by affidavit.
September, Jefferson denied charges in letter to Washington.

1793 May, Washington indicated to Jefferson a wish that Freneau be discharged. But Jefferson in his Anas said, "His paper has saved our Constitution, which was galloping fast into monarchy."
August, in Cabinet meeting, Washington burst out against "that rascal Freneau"--from Jefferson's Anas.
September, yellow fever invaded Philadelphia, stopping business.
October, Freneau resigned as translator. Also, he published the last issue of the National Gazette, on the 26th.
November (?) returned to Monmouth.

1794 Published The Village Merchant, with "The Country Printer," in Philadelphia.
Published The Monmouth Almanac for 1795, at Monmouth.

1795 Published collection of Poems at Monmouth.
May, began publishing the Jersey Chronicle, at Monmouth.

1796 April, printed last issue of the Jersey Chronicle.

1797 March, began The Time Piece, in New York, with Alexander Menut.
September, Menut was replaced by Matthew Davis.

1798 January, retired from The Time Piece, and sailed for Charleston.
March, returned to New York.

1799 March, began "Robert Slender" essays in the Aurora, in Philadelphia.
December, Slender's Letters was published in Philadelphia.

1800 Contributed "Slender's" and other essays to the Aurora.

1801 February, ended the Slender series.

Autumn, resumed sailing as master of the John.

1802 January, returned to New York as master of the Fanny.

1803-1807 Master of the Washington and other ships.

1804 August-September, evidently wrote Slenderesque political essays for the Aurora, mostly as by members of the "Bunker" family.

1807 Retired from the sea because of the Embargo Act.

1809 Supervised printing of Poems at Philadelphia, evidently also contributing essays to the Aurora.

1810-1815 Evidently contributed essays to the Aurora under various pseudonyms, while probably helping to edit and print it.

1815 Published new Poems in New York.

1816-1821 Evidently contributed essays to Aurora, while probably helping edit and print it, signed largely by "Old Soldier." Also contributed scattered poems and essays to the New York Weekly Museum.

1818 Home was destroyed by fire in October, with many manuscripts and letters.

1821-1825 Published many poems and some essays in the True American of Trenton, N. J.

1824 Moved to farm near Freehold, N. J.

1827 Published last known poem printed in his lifetime, on the Battle of Monmouth, in the True American, June 30.

1832 August, applied for federal pension, granted later. December 18, died in snowstorm near his home.

Chapter 1

Introduction

I. Freneau's Fame

As a free-lance writer contributing to newspapers and magazines in New York, Philadelphia, and Charleston, and as author of several pamphlets of verse and two volumes--*Poems*, 1786, and *Miscellaneous Works*, 1788--by 1790 Philip Freneau had achieved a considerable popularity. His poems were republished throughout the nation; his anti-British sentiments were applauded; and his humorous verse was well accepted. One poem, "The Jug of Rum," appeared in dozens of newspapers in 1791 and 1792. "Verses Made at Sea," published in the *Freeman's Journal* for April 13, 1785, was reprinted in ten or more newspapers by 1792. "The Drunken Soldier," in the *Columbian Herald* (Charleston, S. C.) for July 10, 1786, was reprinted at least six times by 1788. "The Virtue of Tobacco," in the *City Gazette* (also Charleston) for June 25, 1786, appeared seven times more by 1792. "Father Dobbin's Complaint," in the same newspaper for January 15, 1790, was republished ten times by 1792.[1] These examples are typical.

As assistant editor to Childs and Swaine on *The Daily Advertiser* in New York, where the first national government was founded under the Constitution, Freneau was close to the politics of the new nation and the efforts of Hamilton, Secretary of the Treasury, to strengthen American credit and stabilize the currency. In this Hamilton succeeded, but was eyed with suspicion by Secretary of State Jefferson and his friends, Madison, Monroe, and other Southerners. They feared he might try to establish a monarchy with Washington as king. At this time John Fenno, aided by Hamilton, John Adams, and other Federalists, founded a conservative newspaper, the *Gazette of the United States.* In its columns Washington, Adams, Hamilton, and other government officials could do no wrong. Jefferson saw that a "republican" or Whig (later Democratic) newspaper was needed as an opposition to Fenno.

When the government moved to Philadelphia, Madison tried to persuade Freneau to locate his projected newspaper there; and Jefferson offered him a part-time translatorship at $250 a year. Eventually, with Childs and Swaine footing the bill, Freneau founded the National Gazette in the new capital. It was a "liberal" paper that opposed Fenno and the Hamilton policies, ridiculing aristocracy, monarchy, and all things British, supporting revolutionary France. Hamilton struck back with charges that Freneau's salary was a bribe to influence his paper to spread Jefferson's ideas, and that Jefferson was its real director. At once politicians lined up on two sides--the Federalists, led by Hamilton; and the Republicans, as the Democrats were first called, led by Jefferson. Thus the American two-party system began.

Despite Freneau's denial of editorial direction by Jefferson, he was called the "great man's tool" and an obedient voice of the mob for democracy--then a dirty word. He fell rapidly in public favor, but continued to speak for the mass of people and for revolutionary France, whose leaders were shocking Europe with their bloody executions. And the National Gazette's criticisms of Federalism, Hamilton, Washington, monarchy, and all things royal or aristocratic--especially Washington's six-horse, ornate coach and footmen--gave Freneau the name of calumniator of the father of his country. Thereafter, he never quite recovered "respectability." Yet his constant, often amusing ridicule of the rich and of aristocratic, monarch-loving ways--of their supposed plot to found an American royalty--put them to shame and made anything savoring of kings and nobles unpopular among common people. Jefferson said that Freneau's paper had saved the Constitution from monarchy.[2]

But the National Gazette, lacking a subsidy, lasted only two years--1791 to 1793. In retirement at home in Monmouth, Freneau printed a third collection of his Poems in 1795. He published an Almanac for that year, and began a rural newspaper, the Jersey Chronicle. In 1797 his Time Piece (New York) proved to be another National Gazette, and aroused more Federalist hatred. From 1799 to 1801, in Duane's Aurora of Philadelphia, he wrote many satirical essays aimed mostly at the Federalists and President Adams. With Jefferson's election to the presidency, he turned again to the sea, retiring in 1807. When Madison became president in 1809, Freneau brought out his most elaborate edition, an illustrated, two-volume Poems. This edition, filled with his old poems and emphasizing patriotism, was popular. But after the War of 1812, his Poems of 1815, new poems, was a sales failure. His patriotism was no longer in fashion, and his verse on deism probably offended church people; readers were turning to new poets and essayists like Bryant and Irving.

He planned a last collection for 1822, to include the best of his poems and essays; but the plan fell through. In a final creative outburst, he published many new poems and a few essays in the True American (Trenton) from 1821 to 1825. Afterwards, his writings were few and scattered. In his last years, he became an almost forgotten author and remained so for many years after his death in 1832. Then, he was considered inferior to the Connecticut "wits" (Trumbull, Dwight, Barlow, Alsop, and others), who wrote brilliant Federalist satires. Gradually, however, his better lyrics came to be treasured as the best American poems before Bryant, as they are today. For his best nature poems, some critics have regarded him as a precursor of Wordsworth.

A dozen or so of these lyrics are well worth preserving, and rank among the best in American poetry, like "The Power of Fancy," "The Beauties of Santa Cruz," "Eutaw Springs," "The Indian Burying Ground," "The Wild Honey Suckle," and "The Lost Louisa." The best is "The Wild Honey Suckle"---

> No roving foot shall find thee here,
> No busy hand provoke a tear.

"The Power of Fancy," very smooth, reminds us of Milton---

> Fancy, to thy power I owe
> Half my happiness below.

"The Indian Burying Ground" laments the passing of the red hunter---

> The hunter still the deer pursues,
> The hunter and the deer--a shade.

It is chiefly on the merit of these lyrics that Freneau is represented in nearly every anthology of American poetry, or literature. He wrote many "poems" that are doggerel, and many others that served as effective satires at the time, but are of small interest now, as are some long poems that approach the epic, like "The Rising Glory of America"---

> A new Jerusalem, sent down from heaven,
> Shall grace our happy earth--perhaps this land,
> Whose ample breast shall then receive, tho' late,
> Myriads of saints, with their immortal king,
> To live and reign on earth a thousand years,
> Thence called Millennium...

Freneau also wrote innumerable essays of various sorts--Addisonian, political, descriptive, humorous, narrative. Many were editorials, often a paragraph or two with the news, serving as comments upon it. These essays have yet to be read by most American-literature scholars, though a large number have recently been made available.[3] But most of the political essays may be ignored as literature; some may be of value to the historian; and a number of the Addisonian, descriptive, narrative, and humorous essays are worth retaining as illustrations of the development of the essay in American literature.

In reviewing Freneau's work and comparing it with those of his contemporaries, only two challenge him in the essay--Franklin and Hopkinson, both of whom had felt the influence of Addison. Franklin is supreme for his time in satirical and utilitarian prose. Hopkinson was more versatile than Franklin, and more humorous than Freneau. Yet in volume and varied types, Freneau outperformed both; and his best poems are easily superior to those of Hopkinson.

Though he remains a minor author, Freneau must be rated as the best writer of eighteenth-century America. His lyrics are among the very best we have. And because he wrote on almost every current subject, he deserves an expanded cultivation in his prose items, which are both numerous and varied. With our present increasing appreciation of our eighteenth-century literature as a background for the blooming of our nineteenth-century writings, Freneau is certain to become the object of more intensive study.

II. Biography

Philip Morin Freneau was born of a French-American father in New York City, on Frankfort Street, on January 2 (old style), 1752. During that year his father, a wine merchant, moved to a farm in Monmouth (now Matawan), New Jersey. His mother was of Scotch ancestry, and he was her first child.

Philip grew up in New Jersey, and attended schools there and in New York, preparing for the ministry, as his father wished. In 1767 his father, Pierre Fresneau (old spelling), died after having lost much of his property. But the widow managed to send Philip to Presbyterian Princeton--then called the College of New Jersey--which he entered as a sophomore, being unusually well prepared in the classics, especially Latin.

In the same year, 1768, John Witherspoon, a vigorous liberal leader, became the new college president. Young Freneau became a friend of Hugh Brackenridge, and later a friend and roommate of James Madison. College life was no grind for him, but a lively, experimental life. He tried writing in many forms of poetry--satires, lyrics, epics--and some prose. At graduation (1771), Brackenridge, an orator, read their joint long poem, "The Rising Glory of America," to hearty applause.

After graduation, Freneau tried teaching and disliked it; then for two years he studied theology, but rebelled at the confinements of orthodoxy. Then he embraced deism, a belief in the scientific, mathematical nature of the universe which operated on natural laws without any miracles.

The colonies' rebellion against England attracted his attention, and in 1775 he wrote several verse satires on the British, poems that later, with other poems, gave him the name "poet of the Revolution." Yet, despite a fervent patriotism, he feared war, and early in 1776 accepted an invitation to sail to the West Indies as guest of a Captain John Hanson, who lived on a sugar plantation in Santa Cruz.

Freneau, who had long dreamed of the beauties and bland climate of the West Indies, remained there over two years, writing and taking some part in privateering raids. Probably feeling remiss for not joining the war for independence, he returned to New Jersey in July, 1778, just after the Battle of Monmouth. There he enlisted as a private in the state militia but saw very little action.

Having learned navigation, he went as a ship captain to the West Indies again and again, meanwhile contributing poems and essays to Brackenridge's United States Magazine (1779). In May, 1780, as a passenger on the privateer Aurora, again bound for the West Indies, he was captured, mistaken for a mate, and imprisoned for six weeks in New York Harbor on a British prison ship and a hospital ship. He suffered severely, and from then on hated the British bitterly.

After recovering at home, Freneau went to Philadelphia and worked as a printer and assistant editor for Francis Bailey, editing The Freeman's Journal from mid-1781 to mid-1782, contributing voluminously then and for several years after. In the fall of 1782 he became a postal clerk in Philadelphia. In 1783 he brought out a translation of Claude Robin's Travels Through North-America. In 1784 he went to sea again.

Bailey published Freneau's first book-size collection of Poems in 1786, and in 1788 a Miscellaneous Works, half poetry and half prose. These books were fairly popular, especially with Huguenot friends in Charleston, South Carolina, where his young brother Peter was a successful business man and state secretary.

In 1789 he retired from the sea, and in 1790 married Eleanor Forman, a neighbor's daughter twelve years his junior, and settled in New York as assistant editor to Childs and Swaine, publishers of the Daily Advertiser. By 1791, he was planning to set up his own newspaper; and presently he was persuaded to do so in Philadelphia, the new national capital, by his friend Madison and financed by Childs and Swaine. To help him defray expenses, Secretary of State Jefferson gave him a part-time place as translator.

In Philadelphia, Fenno's conservative Gazette of the United States dominated the newspapers, praising government officials and supporting all Federalist measures, especially Treasury Secretary Hamilton's fiscal program. Freneau's National Gazette attacked the funding system, the national bank, and the excise taxes. Hamilton became angry and, under pseudonyms, charged that Freneau was a bribed political tool and Jefferson was the real director of the _National Gazette._ Both Jefferson and Freneau denied the charges, and finally Hamilton, faced with his own weak, circumstantial case, and pressed by James Monroe's defense of Freneau and Jefferson, bowed out.

The _National Gazette_ went on to ridicule Federalism and its monarch-loving, speculating aristocrats. Freneau's contributors were Madison, George Logan, John Taylor, John Beckley, James Monroe, and other "Republicans" (early name of the Democrats). Freneau also struck at Britain and all Anglophiles, supported revolutionary France, and condemned Washington's Proclamation of Neutrality early in 1793, at the outbreak of war between England and France. He also championed the new French ambassador, Genet, whose indiscreet remarks caused him to be recalled; fearing to return to bloody France, Genet married an American girl and settled on Long Island.

In September, 1793, yellow fever hit Philadelphia and brought business to a halt. Childs now withdrew his support from the _National Gazette,_ which had never been profitable. Freneau resigned the translatorship and retired to his home in New Jersey.

President Washington had been annoyed by Freneau, and would have been pleased if Jefferson had fired him. But Jefferson said in his _Anas_ for May 23, 1793: "His paper has saved our Constitution which was galloping fast into monarchy." It is now a moot question--would our government have become a monarchy, had there been no Freneau?

In New Jersey, Freneau became his own printer, published an almanac for 1795, a new collection of _Poems_ (1795), and a rural newspaper, the _Jersey Chronicle,_ in 1795-96, again attacking Federalism and Britain and supporting Republicanism and France.

Early in 1797, with a partner, Alexander Menut, Freneau began a newspaper in New York, _The Time Piece._ After six months, Menut withdrew, and Matthew Davis replaced him. _The Time Piece_ became another enemy of Federalism, Britain and President Adams, and a supporter of France. It seemed impossible for Freneau to make money on his projects, however, and he retired, beset by debts, at the end of the year.

By 1799 he had again drifted to Philadelphia, where the _Aurora_, originally published by B. F. Bache, was now run by William Duane, and was more anti-Federalist than the _National Gazette_ had been. Probably Freneau set type and helped edit the newspaper, meanwhile contributing political essays. In 1799 he began a series of satires by "Robert Slender," aimed at Adams, the Federalists, and Britain. A collection of them was published late in the year as _Letters on Various interesting and important Subjects._ "Slender" appeared occasionally in the _Aurora_ till February, 1801, when Jefferson was finally elected President.

With the victory over Federalism, Freneau retired to his farm, and presently went back to the sea. For a few weeks, he evidently participated in the Philadelphia election war of 1804, in a series of twenty political essays aimed primarily at Tench Coxe, by members of the "Bunker" family.

Jefferson's Embargo Act of 1807 forced Freneau off the ocean, and again he settled on the farm, now with four daughters to rear. In 1809 he supervised a two-volume edition of his _Poems_ in Philadelphia, meanwhile apparently helping to publish the _Aurora_ and contributing essays to its columns. Duane, the editor, published almost no poetry.

Occasional Freneauesque essays continued to appear in the _Aurora_ during and after the War of 1812, often attacking the dissenting Yankees and urging a countrywide support of President Madison. In 1815, Freneau published a tiny two-volume edition of new _Poems_ in New York. It was a sales failure, perhaps because the reading public was in no mood for patriotic sentiments in an aftermath of disappointment over the war, and also because the edition contained a number of deistic poems. Deism was then regarded by many orthodox Christians as similar to atheism.

Freneau continued to drift in and out of Philadelphia, apparently continuing to help print and edit the _Aurora_, contributing essays often signed with pseudonyms that had appeared in the _National Gazette._ One was "An Old Soldier," who opposed Britain, Federalism and monarchy, and supported France, democracy and the Democrats. Now Freneau began to condemn the American Indians as dangerous savages, as early in his career he had idealized them and the primitive way of life. At last, it seems, he came to agree with his friend Brackenridge, who saw them realistically.

In 1818 the Freneau home, Mount Pleasant, was burned, and with it many letters and manuscripts. A few years later the family--Freneau, his wife, and two unmarried daughters--settled on a farm near Freehold, New Jersey. He sold parcels of land to pay debts, and did little or no income-producing work. From 1821 to 1824, in a last creative burst, he published many new poems and a few essays in the Trenton _True American._ His last known published poem appeared there in 1827. He had planned a final collection of his works, prose and verse, but the project fell through.

During the summer of 1832, Freneau applied for a federal pension of $35 a month, which was granted. But he was not to enjoy it. On the evening of December 18, 1832, he left the Freehold corner store to walk home in a snowstorm. The next day he was found dead, with a broken hip, in a swamp crossing.

He was buried on the old estate near present-day Matawan, under a rather elaborate stone marked "Poet's Grave."

Notes

1. Lewis Leary, _That Rascal Freneau,_ New Brunswick, N. J., 1941. Here referred to as Leary. He found many examples of reprintings, but there were probably some that he missed.

2. Jefferson's _Anas,_ May 23, 1793.

3. _The Prose of Philip Freneau,_ P. M. Marsh, ed., Scarecrow Press, Metuchen, N. J., 1955; and _A Freneau Sampler,_ P. M. Marsh, ed., Scarecrow Press, Metuchen, N. J., 1963.

Chapter 2

The College Poet

I. Pre-College Background

Philip Freneau grew up marked for the ministry, the profession his father had selected for him; and so his pre-college studies were in line with this goal, the classical languages, especially Latin. His father's death left him free to do as he wished with his studies at Princeton, which emphasized languages, philosophy, and literature. His spare-time reading in the college library evidently developed a great interest in Homer, Virgil, Horace, and the English greats--Shakespeare, Milton, Dryden, Defoe, Addison, Swift, Pope, and Gray.

II. The Undergraduate Poems

In his undergraduate years and shortly after, Freneau was occupied largely in experimental writing, imitating or "improving on" the English writers, trying his hand at the different kinds of verse. In his 1786 Poems he tagged many poems with their dates of composition, and some of the best were done just before or directly after his graduation in 1770.

The first poem in the book, "The Poetical History of the Prophet Jonah," was "done in the year 1768," in heroic couplets like the poems of Dryden and Pope. The second, "The Pyramids of Egypt," was "written in 1770" in blank verse, like Milton's major works. The third, "The Monument of Phaon," bore the date 1770, and is in four-line pentameter stanzas, the first and third and second and fourth lines rhyming, as in Gray's famous "Elegy."

One of his very best lyrics, "The Power of Fancy," resembling Milton's "L'Allegro," is dated 1770, as is "The Citizen's Resolve," which is also in tetrameter couplets. "Epitaph Intended for the Tomb Stone of Patrick Bay" was written in 1769, and is in three-line tetrameter stanzas, one rhyme in each. "Columbus to Ferdinand" was done in 1770, in the form of Gray's "Elegy." "The Rising Glory of America," in its original form a collaboration with Brackenridge, carries the date 1771, and is mostly in blank verse. This is Freneau's version, with Brackenridge's lines deleted.

It is clear that Freneau was writing a great deal in his undergraduate years, experimenting with different forms of poetry, especially during his last year at Princeton, 1770.

Of these early poems, "The Power of Fancy" is easily the best. It is a long poem of 154 lines of tetrameter couplets--a description of Fancy, her nature, activities, and powers, and the poet's worship of her--

This spark of bright, celestial flame
From Jove's seraphic altar came,
And hence alone in man we trace
Resemblance to the immortal race.

Not only is Fancy divine, a sign of man's immortality, but also an all-inclusive power, the essence of all creation--

Ah! what is all this mighty WHOLE,
These suns and stars that round us roll!
What are they all, where'er they shine,
But _Fancies_ of the Power Divine!

Thus the poet conceives the universe as a creation of God's fancy, a deistic idea possibly taken from Addison's version of the 19th Psalm:[1]

The spacious firmament on high,
With all the blue aetherial sky
And spangled heavens, a shining frame,
Their great Original proclaim.

But to Freneau, Fancy is more than a sign of divinity in all things. She walks on the brain and on the moon, descends to Hell, looks on Arcadia, the deserts, and the forests. She flies over the seas to all parts of the globe, she has seen the glory of Greece and Rome, and she bears the poet to the dawn in the far East, to India, Tahiti, and finally to California. She also leads him to the tomb of his sweetheart. In Fancy are "endless images" and to her he owes "half my happiness;" she is the creator of Elysia, the music of Orpheus, and his charming of Pluto. The poet will commune with her alone:

Come, O come--perceiv'd by none,
You and I will walk alone.

The form closely resembles that in Milton's "L'Allegro," which is mostly in tetrameter couplets, and steeped in a similar tone of dreamy wishes for a joyful companionship. It is almost as if Freneau had a volume of Milton before him. In the poem's one footnote, he refers to Paradise Lost; and in the last lines, he mentions "Elysian groves," Orpheus, Pluto, and Euridice (Orpheus's wife).

The other undergraduate poems are undistinguished. "The Prophet Jonah," in some 180 heroic couplets, paraphrases the Bible story; but it may have been a preliminary exercise. "The Pyramids of Egypt" is a blank-verse dialogue between "Traveller" and "Genius," with "Time" providing the conclusion that time brings all things low, that only God is immortal.

"The Monument of Phaon" begins with Sappho lamenting the departed Phaon. In three four-line rhymed pentameter stanzas, like those in Gray's "Elegy," Ismenius tells her he has seen Phaon's grave, and then goes on--now in tetrameter couplets--to say how Phaon is mourned in a foreign land (Sicily), and by another maid, Musidora. Then Sappho--in heroic couplets--blames "faithless Phaon," laments her fate, and leaps from the famed Leucadian Rock to her death.

"The Citizen's Resolve," a comic poem, is a monologue by Lysander, in tetrameter couplets. He longs for the pleasures of love and natural beauty, is bored with the "toll and restless care" of a merchant's life, and ends by leaving his business and going to the "western forests," but--

In three short months, sick of the heavenly train,
In three short months--he mov'd to town again.

"Epitaph Intended for the Tomb Stone of Patrick Bay" has Bay, speaking in three-line, one-rhyme pentameter stanzas, blaming his death on Doctor Rowe, lamenting the pleasures he left behind, and condemning "such infernal quacks."

"Columbus to Ferdinand" is in a favorite stanza, almost Gray's--four pentameters, second and fourth rhymed. It tells the story of Columbus's attempt to persuade the king that there was a new world in the West:

> An unremitting flame my breast inspires
> To seek new lands amidst the barren waves,
> Where falling low, the source of day descends,
> And the blue sea his evening visage laves.

In these poems we find the young poet trying his skills in several verse forms, inclined to imitate his English models, yet varying the forms and the subjects. "The Power of Fancy," a remarkable production for a student of eighteen, shows a wide-ranging imagination, and remains one of the best lyrics in American literature.

III. A Semi-Epic

Freneau's part in the first form of "The Rising Glory of America," written at college with Hugh Brackenridge, is found in A Poem on the Rising Glory of America, published at Philadelphia in 1772. This version omits mention of Washington, damns France and Spain, praises Britain, and hails America as "the seat of empire, the abode of kings."

The poet was to change the poem considerably for the 1786 Poems. There it appears as "written 1771." It was revised for the volume--Brackenridge's part taken out, Washington added as the leader opposing "the bold invaders of his country's rights," the British called a "cruel race," and America viewed as a future "new Jerusalem," happy in the coming millennium.

Like the original, Freneau's "Glory" is done in blank verse and dramatic form, with three speakers--Acasto, Eugenio, and Leander--but it is much shorter, of somewhat over 450 lines, in contrast to 700 in the early form, indicating that the Brackenridge part was about 250 lines. The poem was Freneau's first approach to the epic, and apparently echoes Milton and the translations of Homer and Virgil. It starts:

> Now shall the adventurous muse attempt a strain
> More new, more noble, and more flush of fame
> Than all that went before...

Compare Milton in Paradise Lost, addressing his muse:

. . . I thence
Invoke thy aid to my adventurous song,
That with no middle flight intends to soar
Above the Aonian mount, while it pursues
Things unattempted yet in prose or rime.

Footnote references to Genesis, Horace, and Homer suggest the epic mood in which the poet worked. He pointed to the fact that the glories and heroes of old nations were gone, and that America was about to replace them with greater glories, greater heroes, greater arts, and finally peace:

Lost are they all that shin'd on earth before;
Rome's boldest champions in the dust are laid,
Ajax and great Achilles are no more,
And _Philip's_ warlike son, an empty shade!--
A WASHINGTON among our sons of fame
We boast--conspicuous as the morning star...
--Greece and Rome no more
Detain the Muses on Cithaeron's brow
Or old _Olympus,_ crown'd with waving woods,
Or _Haemus'_ top, where once was heard the harp,
Sweet Orpheus' harp, that gain'd his cause below
And pierc'd the heart of Orcus and his bride...
Hither they wing their way, the last the best
Of countries, where the arts shall rise and grow,
And arms shall have their day--Even now we boast
A _Franklin_...
--and, worse than all,
The fiercer passions of the human breast
Shall kindle up to deeds of death no more,
But all subside in universal peace.

Note

1. _Spectator,_ no. 465.

Chapter 3

Other Poems Before 1780

I. Pamphlet Verse of the 1700's

The young Freneau was very eager to break into print. Shortly after quitting a rural teaching position in Flatbush in the fall of 1771, he placed a manuscript with a New York printer. The tiny collection[1] (twenty-eight pages) featured "The American Village" by "Philip Freneau, A. B."--a touch of vanity. This poem was both an imitation and a reply to Goldsmith's "Deserted Village" (1770), which had achieved great popularity. Goldsmith's poem begins thus:

> Sweet Auburn! loveliest village of the plain,
> Where health and plenty cheer'd the laboring swain,
> Where smiling spring its earliest visit paid,
> And parting summer's lingering blooms delay'd:
> Dear lovely bowers of innocence and ease,
> Seats of my youth, when every sport could please:
> How often have I loiter'd o'er thy green
> Where humble happiness endear'd each scene!

And Freneau's poem begins in this way:

> Where yonder stream divides the fertile plain,
> Made fertile by the labours of the swain,
> And hills and woods high tow'ring o'er the rest,
> Behold a village with fair plenty blest.

Goldsmith's poem is of melancholy, regret, and condemnation of forces that had ruined the village. But Freneau rebukes him with persistent optimism and confidence in the future of America.

> Though Goldsmith weeps in melancholy strains
> Deserted Auburn and forsaken plains,
> And mourns his village with a patriot sigh,
> And in that village sees Britannia die:
> Yet shall this land with rising pomp divine,
> In its own splendor and Britannia's shine.

The other poems in the pamphlet include "Upon a very Ancient Dutch House in Long-Island," in eight four-line stanzas of alternately rhymed pentameter--

> Behold this antique dome by envious time
> Grown crazy, and in ev'ry part decay'd...

The poet imagines the life of the one-time occupants, a Dutch lad and the lass "as thick as she was long," and laments the ruins. Another, "The Miserable Life of a Pedagogue," in tetrameter couplets ridicules the life of a teacher:

> A plague I say on such employment,
> Where's neither pleasure nor enjoyment.

Still another is "The Farmer's Winter Evening, A Poem. To the Nymph I never saw"--about gay life in a cottage, and of Kate, the shepherdess, and wishes for a dream life with her:

> Then I, my lovely maid, shall see thee
> Drinking the deep streams of LETHE...
> And I too will quaff the water,
> Lest it should be said, O daughter,
> Of my giddy, wand'ring brain,
> I sigh'd for one I've never seen.

The group is interesting, showing considerable originality, and the imitation of Goldsmith, among many such, is a creditable performance. The 1772 pamphlet of the "Rising Glory" has been mentioned.

In 1775 Freneau published American Liberty in New York, and republished it in the same year in Philadelphia, as The Present Situation of Affairs in North-America, a pamphlet of eight pages. It is another attempt at the epic, in about 500 heroic couplets, reviewing the background and conditions of the colonies, the beginning revolution, and the Americans' determination to be free, predicting a future land of liberty and happiness:[2]

> Such is the life our foes with envy see,
> Such is the godlike glory to be free.

But there are forebodings of a coming extended conflict, praise for Washington and Warren, contempt for Tories and General Gage, a sneer for Catholic Canada, and shock at the behavior of King George. But it is more a frightened warning than a call to patriotic support of the cause.

In New York and Philadelphia, in the same year, the poet published a twenty-four-page pamphlet, A Voyage to Boston, mostly about the situation in Boston, with ridicule of Gage and other British officers there, and a description of the American camp at Cambridge; it also expresses a hope for reconciliation with Britain--all in heroic couplets:[3]

> Long may Britannia rule our hearts again,
> Rule as she rul'd in George the Second's reign;
> May ages hence her growing empire see,
> And she be glorious, but ourselves be free.

Obviously Freneau was not thinking of independence then.

About the time when Gage was recalled in August, 1775, the poet published an eight-page pamphlet in New York, General Gage's Soliloquy, a supposed confession of sins in heroic couplets. It appears in the 1786 Poems, probably shortened; no copy of the original print is known:[4]

> I speak the language of my heart--shall I
> Steal off by night, and o'er the ocean fly,
> Like a lost man to unknown regions stray,
> And to oblivion leave the darksome day?--
> Or shall I to Britannia's shores again,
> And, big with lies, conceal my thousands slain?

"General Gage's Confession," evidently from a manuscript in Ridgway Library in Philadelphia, has Gage confessing to a friar, "Father Francis," who assures him (a satire on Catholicism) of his safety:[5]

> All should be well--from sins like this, I ween,
> A dozen masses shall discharge you clean;
> Small pains in purgatory you'll endure,
> And hell, you know, is only for the poor.

No new poems by Freneau were published in 1776 and 1777, while he was in Santa Cruz. But in 1778, in Philadelphia, American Independence appeared--evidently as a pamphlet of twelve pages, then with other poems carrying another title, one being The Travels of the Imagination (by J. Murray), another Miscellanies for Sentimentalists, where it is one of seven pamphlets and signed by "Philip F----." The poem is in his favorite form, heroic couplets like Pope's. It begins:

> 'Tis done; and Britain for her folly sighs;
> Take warning tyrants, and henceforth be wise:
> If o'er mankind fate give you sovereign sway,
> Take not the rights of human kind away.

American Independence[6] is an ambitious poem, condemning George III and classing him with Cain, Nero, Herod, and Domitian. It also attacks Tory Professor Cooper of King's College (Columbia), Gage,

Tryon, Burgoyne, Howe, prison ships, Britain, and Tories generally. It praises the King of France, General Gates, and freedom, urging Americans to avenge their wrongs and drive out the tyrants. The form is heroic couplets with a touch of Gray:

Full many a corpse lies rotting on the plain,
That ne'er shall see its little brood again...

It also predicts eventual freedom for America:

Ne'er from thy coasts, Columbia, may she fly,
Prosper and live the favourite of the sky...
America, the works of peace be thine;
Thus shalt thou gain a laurel more divine.

The poem, of over 300 lines, is a shrill call to patriots to crush the British!

II. Other Verse of the 1770's

Freneau's other poems at this time appeared mostly in newspapers and Brackenridge's United States Magazine (1779). "The New Liberty Pole--Take Care" in the Trenton True American (Aug. 17, 1822), in four-line rhymed tetrameter verse, was there noted as having appeared in hand-bill form in 1775; it tells a tale of Whig-Tory fights in New York over a Liberty pole. "Reflections on Gage's Letter to General Washington, of Aug. 13," in the New York Constitutional Gazette (Oct. 18, 1775), appears in the 1786 Poems as "On the Conqueror of America shut up in Boston" in heroic couplets. It says little of Gage, but much in warning Americans against England:[7]

Americans, at freedom's fane adore,
But trust to British clemency no more;
The generous genius of the isle has fled,
And left a mere impostor in his stead--
If conquer'd, rebels, their past records show,
Receive no mercy from this parent foe.

Freneau wrote "Mac Swiggen: a Satire" in 1775; probably it was published in a New York newspaper, but no original is known. Part of it is from one of his college poems aimed at campus Tories. In 1775 it may have been aimed at a New York rival. A raucous satire of about 150 lines in heroic couplets, it still sounds like a college poem:[8]

I interfere not with your vast design---
Pursue your studies, and I'll follow mine...

Its humor sounds like that of a college undergraduate:

Mac Swiggen, hear--Be wise in times to come;
A dunce by nature, bid thy muse be dumb,
Lest you, devoted to the infernal skies,
Descend, like Lucifer, no more to rise.

It seems likely that the poem was finished late in 1775, because already the author was yearning for the West Indies:

Let others here their hopes and wishes end;
I to the sea with weary steps descend...
In distant isles some happier scene I'll choose,
And court in softer shades the unwilling Muse.

In 1776, according to the 1788 version, he wrote "The Jamaica Funeral," in thirty-two rhymed four-line stanzas; but it did not appear until the 1786 Poems came out. It tells a tale of the funeral of Alexander, "the rich, the great, the brave," a pompous funeral attended by a large crowd, some to hear the sermon, some to escape a nagging wife, some to drink the free wine. A parson came, drank, and dunned his parishioners for their dues; a sire who rebuked him was laid low from a blow of the parson's staff. The preacher then stuffed himself at the dinner without saying grace, prayed insincerely over the corpse, and proceeded to preach:[9]

Up to the pulpit strode he with an air,
And from the Preacher thus his text he read,
"More I esteem, and better is by far
A dog existing than a lion dead..."

The purpose is to ridicule the orthodox minister in the person of a hypocrite:

The words of faith in both his hands he bore,
Prayers, cut and dry, by ancient prelates made,
Who, bigots while they liv'd, could do no more
Than leave them still by bigots to be said.

Evidently the poem was written in a bitter moment, marking a period when Freneau was discarding orthodoxy for deism.

In 1779, "Sir Henry Clinton's Invitation to the Refugees" came out as a ballad sheet. Though no original has been found, it is in the 1786 Poems as "Sir Harry's Call." In four twelve-line stanzas, alternating rhymed tetrameter and dimeter lines, it satirizes American Tories who had joined Clinton expecting safety and ease:[10]

Come gentlemen Tories, firm, loyal and true;
Here are axes and shovels, and something to do!
  For the sake of our king,
  Come, labor and sing;

You left all you had for his honour and glory,
And he will remember the suffering Tory:
    We have, it is true,
    Some small work to do...

III. <u>The United States Magazine</u>

Hugh Brackenridge founded <u>The United States Magazine</u> (Philadelphia) in January, 1779, and published it one year as a monthly. He gave it up because of the continuing war and instability of money. To this noble literary experiment, Freneau, recently back from Santa Cruz, contributed several essays and several poems, including some important verse, "The Beauties of Santa Cruz" and "The House of Night." The shorter poems include one probably his but not acknowledged, "The Forsaken Lover," in the October issue; it has nine stanzas like this:

By yonder stream I built a bower,
And deck't it o'er with many a flower,
    The primrose and the violet gay;
The daisies sprung and roses blew
And lofty trees to shade me, grew,
    From Sol's meridian ray.

The four essays are descriptions of the islands--one of Bermuda, one of Santa Cruz (introducing the poem about it), and one of St. James Island. In the June number there is an "Account of a Cave, and a Monument found in it," about a cave in the Bahama island of Eleuthera that Freneau had explored, and of a monument there to a boy buried on the spot, set up in 1770.[11]

"The Beauties of Santa Cruz," one of Freneau's better poems (February), has fifty-two stanzas,[12] preceded by an essay describing the island. The poem begins with an exhortation to a North-American shepherd to leave his "rigorous climes" and come "where never ice congeal'd the limpid stream." In the forty-ninth stanza, the poet again urges the northerner to leave "the bloody plains and iron glooms above;" but, if he must stay, he may "repel the tyrant who thy peace invades." Thus a motive for Freneau's departure from the colonies and for staying out of the conflict is made plain enough.

But most of the poem--in four-line rhymed pentameter stanzas, like those in Gray's "Elegy"--is devoted to describing the island's charms:

> Betwixt the Tropick and the Midway Line,
> In happiest climate lies this envy'd tale;
> Trees bloom throughout the year, flowers ever blow,
> And fragrant Flora wears a lasting smile.

Freneau describes trees, fruits, nuts, fish, the warm sun, rainbows, sweet breezes, and above all the delicious sugar cane, whose charms were so great that

> Whoever sips of this inchanting juice--
> Delicious nectar, fit for Jove's own hall,
> Returns no more from his lov'd Santa Cruz,
> But quits his friends, his country, and his all.

Gray's influence must have been considerable at this time--it is almost as if the poet had the "Elegy" before him for one stanza:

> The drowsy pelican wings home his way,
> The misty night sits heavy on the sea,
> Yon lagging sail drags slowly o'er the main;
> Night and its kindred glooms are nought to me.

The author mentions two flaws in this utopia--hurricanes and slavery--but only briefly in the magazine version. In the 1786 Poems, the slaves' suffering is dwelt on at some length, as is the damage from a recent hurricane.

"King George the Third's Soliloquy" appeared in the May issue, and also in the 1786 Poems, where there are eighty-six lines and a new title, "George III. His Soliloquy for 1779." Both poems are in heroic couplets. Freneau has the King confused, regretting his mistakes, especially the war against America:[13]

> My shatter'd navy pelted, bruis'd, and clubb'd,
> By Dutchmen bullied, and by Frenchmen drubb'd,
> My name abhorred, my nation in disgrace,
> How should I act in such a mournful case!

In the June issue one poem, not acknowledged by Freneau, but probably his,[14] is "King George the Third's Speech to Lord North," in twelve heroic couplets:

> O! North, when first I mounted to the throne,
> I swore to let all foreign foes alone...
>
> But mightier objects lay within my view;
> Old conquests I resign'd, and sought for new...

"The Dying Elm," in the same issue, is in the 1786 Poems--a charming ode in rhymed pentameter, tetrameter, and trimeter with an arrangement and tone like "The Wild Honey Suckle:"

Sweet, lovely Elm, who here dost grow
Companion of unsocial care,
Lo! thy dejected branches die
Amidst this torrid air...
O charming tree! no more decline,
But be thy shades and love-sick whispers mine.

In the July issue was "The Loyalists," in forty-one heroic couplets, ascribed to Freneau by his use of certain lines in other poems denouncing American Tories who opposed the Revolution and fought their neighbors:

But that those monsters, whom our soil maintain'd,
Who first drew breath in this devoted land,
Like famish'd wolves should on their country prey,
Assist its foes, and wrest our lives away:
This shocks belief...

The August issue is notable for the first appearance of Freneau's most ambitious romantic poem, "The House of Night; or, Six Hours Lodging with Death. A Vision." This extravagant tale of the agonizing death of Death contains seventy-three four-line rhymed pentameter stanzas, in Gray's "Elegy" form. Expanded, it reappeared in the 1786 Poems with 136 stanzas. From then on, it seems, Freneau became increasingly dissatisfied with it; his 1795 Poems used only a twenty-one stanza fragment, "The Vision of the Night (A Fragment)," which says nothing of death; portions of the 1786 version were used in other poems. But after 1786, the death of Death and its horrifying atmosphere were dropped. Yet this part is, on first reading, startling and thrilling:[15]

Now from within, the howls of Death I heard
  Cursing the dismal night that gave him birth,
Damning his ancient sire and mother sin,
  Who at the gates of hell accursed brought him forth...

As Death dies, the poet, fleeing the House of Night, sees "a sable chariot drove with wild career," followed by a parade of hellish forms on Death's horses. It is the funeral of Death! As the poet stoops to write an epitaph on the tomb, the vision ends and the sun rises. It was only a dream! He asks, do dreams portend approaching death? And he fatalistically concludes:

Enough--when God and nature give the word,
  I'll tempt the dusky shore and narrow sea,

Content to die, just as it be decreed,
  At four score years, or now at twenty-three.

The last line indicates that Freneau completed the poem in 1775. In the longer 1786 version, he omitted this last stanza, and said that death is only "one unceasing change," that all things "must to ruin go," that the soul seeks "mansions in the starry sphere;" and he concluded more cheerfully:[16]

When Nature bids thee from the world retire,
With joy thy lodging leave, a fated guest
In Paradise, the land of thy desire,
Existing always, always to be blest.

The September issue had Freneau's "Psalm. cxxxvii. Imitated," six six-line stanzas in rhymed tetrameter, dated "Monmouth, September 10, 1779." It is probably a veiled thrust at Britain, ending thus:

Thou Babel's offspring, hated race,
  May some avenging monster seize,
And dash thy venom in thy face,
  For crimes and cruelties like these,
And proof to pity's melting tear,
  With infant blood your walls besmear.

The October issue carried another probable Freneau poem (unacknowledged), "The Forsaken Lover," already mentioned; and in the same issue was "The Sea-Voyage," eight stanzas in much the same form. Leary assigns it to Freneau, though it was not acknowledged, on the basis of Pattee's ascription.[17] There is, however, nothing in the poem about the war or Freneau's anger at Britain, as Leary says.[18] It is a gay thing describing the voyage, a storm, the arrival at "Caesaria's hills," and the poet's reunion with "my charming Caelia:"

From a gay island green and fair
With gentle blasts of southern air,
  Across the deep we hold our way,
Around the barque smooth waters played...

In the December and final issue was Freneau's "Dialogue between his Britannic Majesty and Mr. Fox" (also in the 1786 Poems) a poem of about 250 lines in heroic couplets. Charles Fox, later (1782) foreign secretary, was in 1779 a leader of the Whig opposition to North's policy in America. The King begs for advice:[19]

Good Master Fox, your counsel I implore,
Still George the Third, but potent George no more.
By North conducted to the brink of fate,
I mourn my folly and my pride too late...

Fox at first rejects the plea; the King suggests an alliance of Fox and North; Fox spurns this, the King welters in remorse, and Fox heaps blame on him:

When France and Spain are thund'ring at your doors,
Is this a time for kings to lodge with whores?...

Withdraw your armies from th' Americ' shore,
And vex Columbia with your fleets no more.

Thus we have observed Freneau, just out of college, studying theology and rejecting it, writing a poem on death, fleeing the war for a utopia in Santa Cruz, and experimenting with verse forms --largely in the Pope heroic couplet and the Gray four-line stanza. At first he joined the "rebellion" and attacked Britain, but still hoped for a reconciliation; then he became a revolutionist, yet with no urge for actual combat. Presently his hatred for Britain was to grow into an obsession.

Notes

1. The American Village, New York, 1772.
2. Poems of Philip Freneau, F. L. Pattee, ed., Princeton, 1902, I, 152. Here called "Pattee."
3. From the Philadelphia edition.
4. From the 1786 Poems.
5. Poems of Philip Freneau, Pattee, op. cit., I, 191.
6. In the 1786 Poems as "America Independent."
7. 1786 Poems, p. 85.
8. Ibid., p. 96.
9. Ibid., p. 128.
10. Ibid., p. 261.
11. Also partly in the True American, July 13, 1822. Not in Leary.
12. In the 1786 Poems, the poem has 108 stanzas.
13. From the 1786 Poems.
14. Many poems evidently by Freneau were published in newspapers and magazines, but never signed or acknowledged by him.
15. USM, July, 1779.

16. Notice the resemblance to the close in Bryant's "Thanatopsis."

17. The title changed--in the 1786 Poems, it was "Psalm CXXXVII Versified;" in the 1795 and 1809 Poems, it was "The Jewish Lamentation at Euphrates."

18. Leary, p. 79. See Pattee, I, 293-294.

19. 1786 Poems, p. 177.

Chapter 4

The Poet at His Best, 1780-1790

I. Writings in 1780

1780 was a rather barren year for Freneau the writer. His activities before May are not clear, but he may have been involved financially in the building of a privateer, the Aurora, on which he sailed as a passenger from Philadelphia on May 25 for the West Indies. The ship was captured by a British frigate, and Freneau, found enrolled (by mistake) as a mate, was put on the prison ship Scorpion in New York Harbor, then on the hospital ship Hunter. He suffered severely till released after six weeks. The brutality of his treatment left in him a deep hatred for all things British and he wrote a long, bitter poem, The British Prison Ship, which Bailey published as a broadside, early in 1781, with a short poem, "On the Death of Capt. N. Biddle."[1]

The New-Jersey Gazette (Trenton) published two verse satires on the British, in tetrameter couplets, by "Z.", a Freneau pseudonym, and an unsigned poem, "Dialogue between Satan and Arnold," in alternately rhymed tetrameters.[2] In the December 13 issue of the Gazette appeared "Verse to the Memory of Capt. Nicholas Biddle," attributed by Leary to Freneau. But, signed "W. S.," it was evidently by William Scull, Biddle's first cousin and a poet.[3]

"The British Prison Ship," probably first written in late 1780, is included in the 1786 Poems. It is a long poem of over 600 lines, three cantos in heroic couplets. It tells the story of the ship Aurora, its capture, the removal of the prisoners to New York, the prison ship Scorpion, the hospital ship Hunter, the cruel treatment of the prisoners, and the many deaths. It closes with an appeal to Americans to avenge them, and a condemnation of Britain for her murderous policy. It ends thus:[4]

The years approach that shall to ruin bring
Your lords, your chiefs, your miscreant of a king,
Whose murderous acts shall stamp his name accurs'd,
And his last triumphs more than damn the first.

No doubt it was written from the heart out of a bitter experience, but as a poem it is marred by a strong bias. The best part is found in "Canto I. The Capture," the story of the Aurora, where the gay hopes of the new ship and its poetic passenger are well expressed:

The gay ship now, in all her pomp and pride,
With sails expanded, flew along the tide;
'Twas thy deep stream, O Delaware, that bore
This pile intended for a southern shore
Bound to those isles where endless summer reigns,
Fair fruits, gay blossoms, and enamell'd plains...

But the tone changes--here are some lines about life on the prison ship:

Hail, dark abode! what can with thee compare--
Heat, sickness, famine, death, and stagnant air...

Of the Hessian doctor, Freneau wrote:

By frequent blows we from his cane endur'd
He kill'd at least as many as he cur'd...

And of the captain:

He swore, till every prisoner stood aghast,
And thought him Satan in a brimstone blast...

In the fall of 1780, Benedict Arnold's treason and Major André's hanging as a spy engrossed public attention, and Freneau's. He tried writing a play, half prose, half verse, The Spy, but apparently never finished it. A fragment,[5] missing till recently, has a title, "Act 5. Scene 1. Camp," indicating that the trial of André is about to be portrayed and that the final act was begun. The dialogue of the play is in both blank verse and heroic couplets, and the blank verse is often good. Here is part of a soliloquy by Arnold:[6]

Peace to this gloomy grove that sees me acting
What open day light would disdain to own!---
Ye Woods, be witness to my dark designs
And shade me o'er, ye lofty eminences!
Tremendous Glooms, encompass me around
In clouds that from Greenland's foggy coast
Plutonian darkness on your pinions bring;
Conceal my base intent from human view...

Of further interest is the fact that the manuscript (never published in Freneau's time) contained several songs that Freneau later published partly in his editions of 1786, 1795, and 1809. One of these was "The English Quixote of 1778; or, Modern Idolatry," in ten four-line stanzas of rhymed tetrameter and trimeter, the first three lines (tetrameter) rhyming, and fourth lines rhyming with each other:[7]

> My native shades delight no more;
> I haste to meet the Ocean's roar;
> I seek a wild, inclement shore
> Beyond th' Atlantic Main.

Another song which Pattee says was put into the poem "Mars and Hymen,"[8] untitled in the manuscript, is in eight couplets:

> You chide me and tell me I must not complain
> To _part_ a few days from my favourite swain...

II. _Poems and Prose_, mostly in _The Freeman's Journal_, 1781-1789

Freneau was probably in Philadelphia in the first months of 1781, working for Francis Bailey in some capacity, perhaps learning to set type. Bailey was now expanding his business, and on April 25, 1781, began a new weekly, _The Freeman's Journal._ He was a liberal Whig, like Freneau, so the poet may have begun as a proof reader or typesetter, and then become an assistant editor. An examination of the editorial paragraphs in the _Journal_ indicates that their tone changed on August 1 to a sharper, more literary, Latinized style, Freneau's. He had begun contributing so we may assume that he started editorial work late in July, and continued as "editor" for over a year, and as a contributor much longer. 1781-1782 was his most productive year.

Poetic contributions started with August 8, 1781--"A Poem on the memorable victory obtained by the gallant Capt. Paul Jones, of the Good Man Richard, over the Seraphis," celebrating the famous victory. It appeared in the _Poems_ of 1786, 1795, and 1809.

Many other poems followed, about forty by the end of 1782, thirty from 1783 to 1785, and fifteen from 1786 to 1789. Some survived in fame--"To the memory of the brave Americans" ("Eutaw Springs") and "Verses, made at Sea, in a Heavy Gale"--but most were contemporary, political, and satirical, like "Hugh Gaine's

Life," of a Tory New York editor; "A New York Tory's Epistle;" and "The Progress of Balloons."

More important is Freneau's emergence as an essayist. He had always admired Addison; he apparently owned a set of the Works and a set of the Spectator.[9] It seems he, like Franklin, imitated Addison, though Goldsmith was also an important influence. As managing editor, Freneau wrote editorials and "fillers," mostly essays of description, and presently essays in a series by a world traveller, "The Pilgrim."

"The Pilgrim" is, like Addison's Roger de Coverley, a bachelor, and of about the same age; but he is a lover of wild nature, a primitivist, and a critic of civilization. He has travelled all over the world, is a great lover of republicanism, and has come to see its great symbol, the United States. He lives in a forest north of the city, but comes into town to observe civilization and to criticize it. Gradually, as the essays continue, the Pilgrim becomes less a primitivist and more a man-about-town; his topics were now the manners, morals, and politics of Philadelphia.

There are nineteen numbers in the series, appearing from November 21, 1781, to August 14, 1782. The first eleven came only a week apart, till February. Afterwards, the author's interest lagged. No. XIII (February 20) discussed city politics; No. XIV (May 8) commented on the vanities of ladies and beaus; No. XV (May 29) talked about Tories and Tory words. The subject of No. XVI (June 19) was the irrationality of war; No. XVII condemned lawsuits and lawyers; No. XVIII (July 24) talked of the pettiness of city people; and the last, No. XIX (August 14, 1782), was about cruelty to animals. The writer's interest in primitive life had weakened, and had been replaced by an interest in city life, an Addisonian trait.

But the first essay is a sermon for primitivism and republicanism, and is dominated by a biography of the "author," the Pilgrim. He begins thus:

> Having taken some pains for a considerable time, in my present retired situation, to obtain a sight of such public papers as are periodically printed on this continent, I could not but observe, that there is scarcely

> one which ever presents the reader with any other essays than such as immediately relate to politics, and the transactions of the times, or local and domestic matters, arising from a variety of circumstances in the constant intercourse of men and business. Morality and refined sentiment are shamefully neglected... the author... observing your publication to be conducted upon very liberal principles, proposes to send you, weekly, a collection of such sentiments as may be worth the notice of men of taste.

Having provided a reason for the venture, he proceeds to tell the story of his life:

> I drew my first breath upon the borders of Switzerland .... My father and mother dying, their little estate fell to me....

The story goes on to explain that the Pilgrim, a descendant of William Tell, had always loved republics and hated monarchies:

> I have an innate love for republics, and could never be long at ease in the vicinity of kings, emperors, kingdoms or aristocracies, which, in my opinion, are but different words for tyrants and tyranny.

He goes on to tell of leaving his homeland because of aristocratic neighbors who cut down a lovely forest, and confesses his love of the primitive life:

> There is something in woods and solitudes congenial to my nature; palaces and towns are my abhorrence... by intervals I retired to the forests, and conversed with the simple genius of the wilderness.

The young man set out on travels to Palestine, Tripoli, Naples, Brazil, and many other countries in all parts of the world. Attracted by the "fame of these new republics," he had come to America two years ago.

> I have fixed my place of residence in the midst of a very large forest, not many leagues from the city... I am now in the fifty-sixth year of my age... am engaged in composing a voluminous treatise... De Anima Mundi... I subsist wholly upon roots and vegetables... I have not had an hour's sickness these forty years past, am altogether devoid of ambition, and have never experienced the least inclination to shed the blood of any man, or injure him in the slightest degree. My benevolence is is unbounded, and extends even to the meanest of the

insect creation.

He describes himself as a lover of all men and animals and an enemy to kings, ambitious men, all war and bloodshed, even the eating of flesh. To add to the interest of his introduction, he describes his forest home as a cavern and grotto near a stream, and himself as "considerably above the middle size," very swarthy, accustomed to walking with a black ebony cane, wearing spectacles, and speaking most of the world's languages. He warns people not to try to find him; if discovered, he will leave the country.

Thus Freneau introduced his fictional character, much as Addison had done with his "Spectator." Essays III (Dec. 5, 1781) and IV (Dec. 12) describe a rural parson and his simple life, a further attempt to "sell" primitivism. No. VI (Dec. 26) dwells on solitude, death and sleep, and war. No. VII (Jan. 2, 1782) discusses the folly of duelling. No. XII (Feb. 13, 1782) criticizes formal education and praises the advantages of rural life. And so six of the essays develop a primitivist philosophy.

Essays II and V ridicule English eccentricities; VII is an oration on America's greatness, without relation to the other numbers; and IX, X, XI, XIII, XIV, XV, XVI, XVII, and XVIII discuss subjects that city people talk about--servants, books, the stage, formal education, political disputes, fashions, Tories, war's irrationality, and the pettiness of city people. The last, No. XIX, has a relation, perhaps, to primitive matters; it discusses cruelty to animals. As a whole, the series fails to live up to the expectations aroused by the introduction. More than half the essays resemble those of the Tatler or the Spectator, with letters from fictitious correspondents, comic situations, etc. For example, note the content of No. IX (Jan. 16, 1782):

> That I may not be deemed inattentive to, or neglectful of such epistles as are transmitted to me by several new correspondents, I shall in this paper insert two or three I lately received...
>
> Mr. Pilgrum,
> I am very glad that you did not axcept that there shallenge from Mr. Simple... Supos you should fite him,--why then you fite him. Well then, he kils you or you

> kils him, thers an end of you, if you kils him, you will be hang'd... let it be whitch it wil, we shal never se that bigg book of yours about the Animal Mundy... ever since we have been in this town, my mistrus has spent the evening out, and she stais there sum times til five o'klok in the morning... I and the horses stay in the rane...
>
> ELIAKIM STOUT,
> Koachman to Mrs. Margery Fidget...
>
> I thank Mr. Eliakim for his good opinion of me in regard to Jonathan Simple, and desire he will not trouble himself... but as to Mrs. Margery Fidget, she must be destitute not only of benevolence, but common humanity...

This is a far cry from essays on a primitive way of life, and clearly the product of a city mind, similar to the Tatler and Spectator essays by Steele and Addison.

The oration about America in No. VIII, unlike any other essay Freneau ever wrote, likewise has no affinity with primitivism:[10]

> When Nature first brought forth her infant the American world, to enjoy the blessings and vivifying influences of the new created sun, as if conscious of the injuries this part of her creation was to suffer in future ages, she seemed particularly industrious; she took especial care to place it in such a situation that many centuries, an immense number of years, must elapse before it could possibly be discovered by the natives of the eastern continent... ages rolled away; the old world was unpeopled, and peopled again: Nations grew and flourished; they quarrelled, and fought, and made peace: The four great monarchies succeeded each other and fell again into decay...
>
> In the process of time... this immense continent was at length raised from its long night of obscurity.... As the Europeans had the means, they of course conceived they had the right to extirpate the innocent natives, or drive them from the sea coasts to the interior parts... Britain seemed very busy in banishing and expelling her subjects to this remote region... These, with a mixture of adventurers from various nations, at length humbled the savage tribes... Britain soon cast a greedy eye upon the hard earned possessions of this exiled race; she claimed them as subjects, took them under her protection, but said in her heart, "They shall here-

> after be my slaves"... but nature disregarded the connection, and... said, "The union cannot be lasting."--Her words have proved true...
>
> It is not easy to conceive what will be the greatness and importance of North America in a century or two... Agriculture, the basis of a nation's greatness, will here probably be raised to its pinnacle of perfection... commerce will so agreeably and usefully employ mankind, that wars will be forgotten... The iron generations will verge to decay, and those days of felicity advance, which are so beautifully described by the prophetic sages of ancient times.

Freneau's "clairvoyance" was too optimistic, too rural, too Rousseauistic to be close to reality. But he was in love with the mighty Mississippi, the prince of rivers, "in comparison of whom a Nile is but a Rivulet and the Danube a mere ditch;" and with the Great Lakes, and the vast expansion that these navigable waters would facilitate. To him, it was folly for Britain to think she could reduce such an immense continent to her "absolute sway!"

Meanwhile Freneau was writing other essays or editorials for the Journal: on English stubbornness (Aug. 21, 1781); British resemblances to oldtime Mexicans (Oct. 17); refuting Silas Deane (Nov. 14, Dec. 5); denying that Americans were English (Dec. 12); the need for England to suffer a full defeat (Jan. 23, 1782); satire on the Tories Rivington and Odell (Jan. 23); rebuke of Francis Hopkinson for favoring a Tory (March 6); the need for a navy (April 17, 24); the British plans to subjugate America (May 22); criticism of English credulity (June 26); description of a fictional talk between Warren and Pitt (July 3); satire of women's fashions (July 10, 24); defense of American soldiers (Aug. 7, 21); satire on tax grumblers (Aug. 14); suggestion to expel Tories (Aug. 28); description of the city market house, and Bermuda (Sept. 4); salvation for all (Sept. 11, Nov. 27); description of a new edition of the Bible and satire on "great men" (Nov. 20), the power of oratory (Dec. 4); and a satire on the folly of nicknames (Dec. 11). Freneau's range was very wide.

He was now using pseudonyms profusely: "A Republican," "K.," "Orestes," "Hermes," "K. V.," "Christopher Clodhopper,"

"Priscilla Tripstreet," "Virginius," "Martinus Scriblerus," "Jacob Whissel," "Hawser Trunnion," "W. H.," "Harpax," "A. B.," "Catholicus," "G.," "Plus Ultra," and others.

He continued to contribute essays to the Journal in 1783, 1784, and 1785, resuming in 1787, and dropping off in 1788, when he was visiting his brother Peter in Charleston and contributing to papers there.

Many of his essays attacked the British or Tories; others discussed a variety of subjects--the need for a navy, ladies' fashions, Bermuda, a new Bible, a writer's problems, burial places, oratory, nicknames, etc. As time passed, he wrote less about the war and the hated British, and more about the concerns of Philadelphians. He wrote much as Addison might have written, on the affairs and gossip of a well-informed city dweller--the Sabbath, republics, British debt collectors, sleep, despotism, laws and lawyers, the stage, freedom of the press, literary taste, a sailor's problems ashore, the soul, literary ambitions, new inventions, Noah Webster, etc.

As he wrote more essays, Freneau improved his prose style, doing some pieces closely resembling Addison, and he allowed Bailey to assemble many in The Miscellaneous Works (1788). He also translated a book.[11]

In late 1785 and early 1786, he published a dozen poems in Charleston, mostly in the Columbian Herald, from September, 1785, to July, 1786, which included his best lyric, July 6, 1786, "The Wild Honey Suckle." November, 1787, another fine lyric, "The Indian Burying Ground," was published in The American Magazine, Mathew Carey's magazine. In 1788-89, several more poems were printed in the Charleston City Gazette. Meantime, he wrote "New Year's Verses" for the boys who delivered newspapers. Late in 1789 he began to contribute to the New York Daily Advertiser.

In December, 1789, Freneau retired from the sea, sailed from Charleston to New York, and soon was at work on the Daily Advertiser. He married and settled in New York as an editor of the paper, with similar duties, apparently, to those he had had with Bailey on The Freeman's Journal.

The 1780's thus were a period when the poet became an essayist, yet continued to contribute poems to newspapers. Also, in 1786 and 1788, he saw his poems and prose collected and published in real books. These books confirmed his repute as a writer, and now he enjoyed a respectable national reputation.

III. The 1786 Poems

In 1786, while Freneau was at sea, Bailey published the poet's first real book, The Poems of Philip Freneau, "written chiefly during the late war." Bailey, evidently acting as editor, in an "Advertisement" dated June 1, said the contents had been left in his hands by the author, "above a year ago," with permission to publish whenever he thought the time appropriate. The book contained 110 items, including six "New Year's" poems, and also the long ones, "The Rising Glory of America," "The House of Night," "The Beauties of Santa Cruz," "America Independent," "The British Prison Ship," "The Political Balance," "Rivington's Reflections," "Hugh Gaine's Life," and "Rivington's Confession." Gaine and Rivington were Tory printers in New York.

The volume was well printed on good paper; the print remains clear today. But it does not contain Freneau's best work. It includes most of his long, semi-epic poems; its satires are interesting. But the poems of more lasting value are short--"The Power of Fancy," "Eutaw Springs," and "Verses Made at Sea." He was to do his best lyrics from 1786 to 1789, while still a free lance, free from political conflict and untouched by unpoetic contemporary influences.

The last two poems in the book, "Sketches of American History," are a flippant survey from the time of the aborigines to the 1660's, when Britain took the Dutch possessions in America, closing with a prophecy--

> Fate saw--tho' no wizzard could tell them as much--
> That the crown, in due time, was to fare like the Dutch.

The author made a satiric thrust at civilization generally:

> These Indians, 'tis certain, were here long before ye all,
> And dwelt in their wigwams from time immemorial;
> In a mere state of nature, untutor'd, untaught,

They did as they pleas'd, and they spoke as they thought--
No priests they had then for the cure of their souls,
No lawyers, recorders, nor keepers of rolls;
No learned physicians vile nostrums conceal'd--
Their druggist was nature---her shop was the field.

Until middle age, Freneau, fascinated by Rousseau, was a "theoretical" primitivist, romanticizing the Indian and idealizing the simple, "natural" life; and like Rousseau, he never deserted the city for the woods. He was too much a product of culture and formal education to leave that milieu.

IV. The Miscellaneous Works, 1788

In 1788, encouraged by the modest success of the 1786 volume, Bailey brought out the second Freneau book, half prose, half poetry--The Miscellaneous Works of Mr. Philip Freneau. It was a subscription project: 28 subscribers in Pennsylvania, New Jersey, and Delaware; 88 in New York (including 2 from South Carolina, 1 from New Jersey, and 1 from Kentucky); 31 from Maryland; and 234 from South Carolina, mostly Charleston, making a total of 381. Some ordered two or more copies. The names included many of distinction: Charles Biddle, Mathew Carey, Peter Markoe, David Rittenhouse, De Witt Clinton, Edward Livingston, John Pintard, Charles Pinckney, Ebenezer Hazard, James Carroll, Aedanus Burke, Peter Freneau, George Logan, David Ramsay, several Congressmen, and others. Evidently no attempt was made to solicit subscribers in Virginia, Georgia, or New England.

The essays were mostly new but also included several from the Pilgrim series, in a new grouping called "The Philosopher of the Forest" (eleven numbers), the "Philosopher" being merely another name for the "Pilgrim." Many prose pieces are by "Robert Slender," a fictional weaver who resembled Brackenridge--tall, independent, eccentric.

"Slender" is a satirist, discoursing on the folly of literary ambitions, ridiculing debtors and creditors, tutors, poets, bachelors, sailors, lawyers and lawsuits, literary traditions, romantic love, Tories, and Rivington's Royal Gazette of New York.

Several of the "essays" are short stories; "The Splenetic Indian," a tale of an educated redman who turned back to primitive life and liquor; "Report of a Law Case," a comic tale of a lawsuit; "Light, Summer Reading," a story of a futile love and extravagant romance; "The Sailor's Relief," a humorous story of a sailor's troubles ashore; and "A Discourse on Esquires, with a Short Narrative," a satiric treatment of pompous public officers.

"Philosopher of the Forest, Num. VIII" is a dream essay satirizing literary traditions, resembling Addison's "Visions of Mirzah."[12] The dreamer is transported to a large plain, the Walk of Human Life, then to the Temple of Oblivion, whose superintending spirit tells him all people are doomed to pass through the temple. He guides the dreamer to the Palace of Fame, sought by all; there people make futile attempts to be remembered. The "Genius of the Temple" constantly blows a trumpet, and the ambitious people's labels are blown away.

> Thus it is then, said I, that mankind are the sport of endless deceptions; "Tell me, kind spirit, for what wise purpose could man have been designed, and why is he continued in his present state of existence merely to be actuated by desires which were never meant to be gratified... ?"
>
> "The miseries of your species," replied the spirit, "are principally owing to the suggestions of the spirit of pride. What is the race of man, that they should be panting for habitations beyond the stars! You imagine yourselves the most curious work of the Deity because you possess five distinct senses--Believe me, there are beings in the universe that possess as many thousands. The qualifications that Nature designed for man in his present state, are ever in his power. It is by seeking for things that are beyond him... that he becomes miserable..."

Another dream essay, "The Academy of Death" has a similar beginning. The dreamer finds himself in a long avenue ending in darkness, leading to life after death. Soon it leads him to a pleasant land and a building labelled "This is the Academy of Death." The doors are inscribed with great names, and the dreamer is led to several that open at the superintendent's command. One is Plato's:

> He was sitting on a bench, and looking horizontally, as if meditating on something future; at the same time holding imaginary dialogues with his master Socrates, who was not present.---"You may think what you will of it, Socrates," said he (musing) "but I will honestly confess that I was an enemy to the poets, and ordered them to be banished from my visionary commonwealth, only because I failed in my early endeavors to make poems equal to those of Homer..."

Then Alexander's door was opened:

> Alexander was engaged in conversation with an odd looking ghost, whom I recalled... to be no other than Diogenes---"Tell me, Sawny," said the Cynic (with a malicious grin), "were you sincere when you said you would wish to be Diogenes in preference to all other men, had you not happened to be Alexander?"
>
> "I was so far sincere," replied the conqueror, "that, had it not been my lot to be born a king... I should have wished to have been born a philosopher, that I might, in like manner, play the tyrant with their minds."

Aristotle was disgusting with his malignity, choler, impatience, and dogmatism. Homer's appearance was vulgar, but he proved affable and talkative. Disillusioned about fame and dying in poverty, he had sung fragments of his poems for an existence, and now he revealed an interesting secret:

> "... Ulysses might have returned home in less than the tenth part of ten years, had Penelope been really the model of conjugal virtue I have pictured her. Alas, poor man, that was not the case!---She was, in fact, one of the most noted termagants and jilts of her age, and the poor wanderer remained abroad... that he might be out of hearing of her tongue..."

As to Helen of Troy, Homer said that she was tired of her elderly husband, who bored her by always dressing in blue.

> "... Paris, on the contrary, was a young fellow, and never appeared habited in any other than superfine scarlet. That circumstance was sufficient to turn the scale of female affection in his favour."
>
> Here the governor stamped his foot, and the door closed: "You must have no further conversation with Homer," said he; "what he has been telling you are secrets that ought not to be divulged..."

Freneau's humor was wont to tease the ladies about their

fashions. Replying to "Christopher Clodhopper," who had criticized odd fashions, male and female, and had advocated taxing high heels and gilt buttons, "Priscilla Tripstreet" retorted:

> Avaunt, ye *Clodhoppers* of the age! enjoy in peace your wretched fare and still more wretched attire, but come not henceforward into public view with your execrable croakings, to do your utmost to rob us of our teas and our sugars, our calashes and our shoe heels, and other blessings, which, if with-held, as your niggardly hands are itching to do, would render life itself an insupportable burthen.

The Miscellaneous Works contains a variety of essays, even characters like "The Market Man" and "The Debtor." Freneau liked to set up rules of different sorts for special situations, like "Rules and Directions, How to Avoid Creditors, Sheriffs, Constables, &c." and "Directions for Courtship." His comic tale in diary form of a sailor's dilemmas ashore is one of his best, titled "The Sailor's Relief," supposedly by "Alexander Dismal, Inn-holder."

> January 3, 1785. Find myself woefully in debt already ---dream every night of old *Carlisle,* and other pickaroon constables.---*Mem.* to keep a good look out from my tops, and if possible steer clear those cutter built sons of whores till the river opens.---Jan. 5. At 12 last night, fell in with a watchman, the new building then bearing due west, and Christ church steeple nearly south east. As bad luck would have it he carried no lanthorns, so that he suddenly boarded me in the dark, and at the first shock carried away all the breast hooks of my new blue jacket, the starboard lifts of my half worn castor hat, and nearly two thirds of the after leech of my old great coat. *Note,* he battered my jull severely, but I suspect his main top was somewhat the worse of the judicious and masterly discharges I made upon it with my short oaken cudgel...

"The Voyage of Timberoo-Tabo-Eede, an Otaheite Indian" satirizes the whites' assumption of superiority over the redmen. In it the Tahitians claim sovereignty over the English and sneer at their customs. "On City Burying Places" ridicules the practice of burying corpses in churches. The last number of the *Philosopher* inveighs against war; it is an example of Freneau at his most serious:

> There is nothing that detracts so much from the character of *rationality* that some men are perpetually talking

> of, as distinguishing the human species from the inferior ranks of created beings, than the practice of the savage profession of war, which has constantly vitiated the morals of mankind, misled their understandings, promoted a spirit of pride and barbarity, and rendered irksome and unwelcome to the far greater part of them that small portion of time which was certainly lent us for nobler ends...

Freneau blamed monarchies largely for wars--"monarchs are the children of discord." Was man a rational creature? Or was he doomed to everlasting enmity, till "the soul of the universe, the great principle of harmony and beauty, shall again move upon the superficies of these troubled waters, and bring light out of darkness, beauty and regularity from confusion, darkness and disorder."

The poetic half of Miscellaneous Works contains some of Freneau's best work. "The Pictures of Columbus," another semi-epic work, embraces eighteen separate poems, each telling part of the explorer's life--"Columbus making Maps," "The Call of an Inchantress," "The Mirror," "Columbus addresses King Ferdinand," "Ferdinand and his First Minister," "Columbus addresses Queen Isabella," "Queen Isabella's Page of Honour writing a reply to Columbus," "Columbus at the Harbour of Palos, in Andalusia," "A Sailor's Hut, near the Shore," "Bernardo, a Spanish Friar, in his canonicals," "Orosio, a Mathematician, with his scales and compasses," "Columbus and a Pilot," "Discontents at Sea," "Columbus at Cat Island," "Columbus in a Tempest on his return to Spain," "Columbus Visits the Court at Barcelona," "Columbus in Chains," and "Columbus at Valladolid."

The forms of these poems differ widely: alternately rhymed tetrameters and rhymed couplets in four-line stanzas; blank verse; heroic couplets; nine-line stanzas of tetrameters and trimeters rhymed abab ccdda; and alternately rhymed pentameters in six-line stanzas, as in the final poem, "Columbus at Valladolid." The admiral had retired to die in this town:

> The winds blow high: one other world remains;
> Once more without a guide I find the way;
> In the dark tomb to slumber with my chains--
> Prais'd by no poet on my funeral day,

Nor even allow'd one dearly purchas'd claim--
My new found world not honor'd with my name...

Much of the verse is in dramatic form, as Columbus talks with an enchantress, Ferdinand with a royal minister, a sailor with his wife, Columbus with a pilot, or with Ferdinand and Isabella. The whole poem closes with Columbus in a soliloquy. Freneau sympathized intensely with the great explorer's plight and tragic end. The poem was reprinted, with minor omissions, in the editions of 1795 and 1809. It is certainly one of his better performances, as well as an interesting *tour de force.*

His pessimism about the unwisdom of writing poetry is expressed in "On the Folly of Writing Poetry," addressed to "Sylvius."[13]

Of all the fools that haunt our coast
The scribbling tribe I pity most:
Theirs is a standing scene of woes,
And theirs no prospect of repose.

...

To all that write, and all that read,
Death shall, with hasty step, succeed;
Even *Shakespeare's* page of mirth and tears
Shall sink beneath this flood of years.

Freneau's habitual melancholy over the lack of opportunity for American writers was given further expression in "An Author's Soliloquy"--[14]

My leaves bound up, compact and fair,
In neat array at length prepare:
To pass their hour on time's broad stage,
To meet the surly critic's rage,
The statesman's slight, the pedant's sneer--
Alas! were these my only fear
I should be quiet and resign'd--
What most torments my boding mind
Is that no critic will be found
To read my works and give the wound!

...

Thrice happy DRYDEN, who could meet
Some rival bard on every street:
When all were bent on writing well,
It was some credit to excel...

"Lines written at Port-Royal," a commemorative poem, laments in heroic couplets the destruction by earthquake (1692) of that handsome port:[15]

> Tho' lost to us, PORT-ROYAL claims a sigh,
> Nor shall the Muse the unenvied gift deny...
>
> What now is left of all thy boasted pride!
> Lost are thy glories that were spread so wide;
> A spit of land is thine, by heaven's decree,
> And wasting shores that scarce resist the sea...

Freneau's best lyric, "The Wild Honey Suckle," graces the pages of Miscellaneous Works. A nature poem long before Wordsworth and Bryant, it has long been the reason for calling Freneau the precursor of the romantic, nature-loving poets in English and American literature of the early nineteenth century. Yet it is doubtful that he influenced them much. First published in the Columbian Herald for July 6, 1786, this lovely lyric, according to Leary, "placed Freneau... chronologically at the head of America's procession of poets."[16] Leary says further that Freneau left "the path cut wide by Pope and his imitators to sing in the spirit of the renaissance of wonder." The poem still ranks among the best of American lyrics;[17] the first of four stanzas follows:

> Fair flower, that dost so comely grow,
> Hid in this silent dull retreat,
> Untouch'd thy honey'd blossoms blow,
> Unseen thy little branches greet:
> No roving foot shall find thee here,
> No busy hand provoke a tear.

Almost as memorable is "The Indian Burying Ground" (short title), also regarded as one of Freneau's best lyrics. Its ten stanzas are usually found in general anthologies that include his most representative works:[18]

> In spite of all the learn'd have said
> I still my old opinion keep;
> The posture that we give the dead
> Points out the soul's eternal sleep.
>
> Not so the ancients of these lands;--
> The Indian, when from life releas'd,
> Again is seated with his friends,
> And shares again the joyous feast.

Here, still an aged elm aspires,
Beneath whose far projecting shade
(And which the shepherd still admires)
The children of the forest play'd.

...

By midnight moons, o'er moistening dews,
In vestments for the chace array'd,
The hunter still the deer pursues,
The hunter and the deer--a shade.[19]

And long shall timorous Fancy see
The painted chief, and pointed spear,
And *reason's self* shall bow the knee
To shadows and delusions here.

At a time when short stories were rare, Freneau wrote "Light, Summer Reading," a 7,000-word tale satirizing the romantic novel, about a sad youth madly in love with an insane girl. The lad writes "To Marcia" over-romantic verse in the "Honey Suckle" form; and the tone is similar:

So drooping hangs the fading rose
When summer sends the driving shower,
So to the grave *Marcella* goes,
Her whole duration but an hour:
   Who shall oppose the sad decree,
   Or what, fair maid, recover thee!

The book closes with "A Journey from Philadelphia to New-York," by "Robert Slender"--a comic verse story that Bailey had printed as a pamphlet a year before, over 600 lines of tetrameter-couplet doggerel in four cantos.

On the whole, *Miscellaneous Works* is an entertaining collection. In it are several of Freneau's best poems, and a half dozen essays well worth preserving. In the prose Freneau demonstrated his humor, often very good, and his debt to Addison; and two of the poems are really memorable: "The Wild Honey Suckle" and "The Indian Burying Ground."

Some of his writings in 1789 show him thinking romantically about a lady--"Stanzas written at Baltimore...to Cynthia," in the *Freeman's Journal,* January 29; "Lines Written at Sea, Addressed to Miss -----, New Jersey," in the *Daily Advertiser* for April 15, and "To Harriot," in the *City Gazette* for November 30--all written, it seems, with his fair young neighbor, Eleanor Forman, in mind. This year he also contributed several other poems to the City Gazette. Leary notes a humorous essay in that paper for December 30, reprinted in the Daily Advertiser of New York later, on the use of words.[20] This is probably Freneau's work. But none of these items, apparently, has any lasting value.

Notes

1. Leary confuses this poem with "Verse to the Memory of Capt. Nicholas Biddle," by William Scull, New-Jersey Gazette, Dec. 13, 1780. Leary, p. 424. Freneau's poem is in the 1786 Poems, pp. 166-168.

2. NJG, Sept. 6, Nov. 15, Nov. 1, respectively. "Z." also wrote a letter to Clinton in New York, criticizing his management of the war and his treatment of André, Oct. 18, 1780.

3. See William B. Clark's Captain Dauntless, Baton Rouge, 1949, pp. 251-252; it is a biography of Biddle. This poem and Freneau's on Biddle are quite different.

4. 1786 Poems, p. 206.

5. From Autographs and Documents of Famous Am. Authors, property of Dr. Fisher of Detroit in the 1950's. See P. M. Marsh, "A lost Fragment of Freneau's The Spy," Journal of the Rutgers University Library, June, 1950.

6. Freneau's ms. The Spy, Rutgers University Library. See Pattee for a printed version.

7. In the 1786 Poems, with twelve stanzas, p. 281. Originally printed in The Freeman's Journal for June 26, 1782, with fifteen stanzas; later, in 1795 and 1809 Poems.

8. Pattee, II, 56, note.

9. Leary, pp. 414 and 417.

10. FJ, Jan. 9, 1782.

11. In 1783, Freneau published his translation of Claude Robin's New Travels Through North-America, a French chaplain's observations of the United States in 1781, published in Philadelphia in 1783, and Boston in 1784, with some footnotes by Freneau.

12. Spectator No. 159.

13. MW, pp. 38-41. Not noted in Leary.

14. MW, p. 170.

15. MW, p. 176.

16. Leary, p. 144.

17. MW, p. 152.

18. Ibid., p. 188.

19. Thomas Campbell borrowed this line for his poem, "O'Connor's Child."

20. Leary, p. 384, note 101.

Chapter 5

The Political Journalist, 1790-1800

The New Government and the Constitution

With the beginning of the first national government under the Constitution, there were supposedly no parties, no party-chosen candidates, and no party-inspired laws. There was only one candidate for President--George Washington--and he was elected unanimously. His choice of Cabinet members was non-partisan: Knox, Jefferson, Hamilton, and Randolph. They had to form policies without precedents to guide them, to solve departmental problems by themselves, and to approve or disapprove new national issues. Problems at first emerged mostly from Hamilton's Treasury office--validation of the currency, creation of a funding system for the debt, assumption of state war debts by the national government, an excise tax, and later a national bank. Differing opinions on these issues led to the formation of a democratic "Republican" party opposing Hamilton, who became "boss" of the conservatives, called Federalists, supporters of the Constitution and Washington. At first the Republicans, called Anti-Federalists, were chiefly those who had fought against the ratification of the Constitution. Later, led by Jefferson, they were known as Republicans, and still later as Democrats.

The Constitution was Congress's first major problem. How should its principles be interpreted into law? Members were meeting in New York when Freneau landed there in February, 1790. Evidently he had an understanding with Childs, whose _Daily Advertiser_ he began editing in March.

I. The 1790 Poems

The _Advertiser_ columns began to feature Freneau's poems early in the year: one in January, one in February, twelve in March, two in April, three in May, three in June, and three in July.

Among the subjects are the Long Island Dutch, Rhode Island, the demolition of Fort George, the sleep of plants, the move of Congress to Philadelphia, and the death of Franklin. Freneau, interested in the background of the states, wrote about them with a historical viewpoint, as if planning an epic. His intent is clear from a note with "A View of Rhode Island,"[1] which says the item is extracted from "a new poem, entitled the Rising Empire, not yet published." The Rhode Island poem is in heroic couplets:

> Wash'd by surrounding seas, and bold her coasts,
> A grateful soil the fair Rhode Island boasts...

"A Descriptive Sketch of Maryland"[2] uses the same form, as do "A Description of Pennsylvania"[3] and "A View of Massachusetts;"[4] in the latter the poet shows his spleen:

> Fictitious wants all thoughts of ease control;
> Proud independence sways the aspiring soul...

The intended unity of the whole is revealed in the heroic couplets of "Description of Connecticut"[5] and in "Descriptive Sketch of Virginia:"[6] quoted below:

> Full of her ancient claims, where all is new,
> Vast in her bound, Virginia swells to view:
> First in imagin'd rank she long has stood,
> Built the first town, and first explor'd the wood...

Freneau liked to lament over a ruined building, as in "The Ruins of a Country-Church (A real Picture.),"[7] using the form of Gray's "Elegy," and also satirizing:

> Secure from dreams, that vex the midnight hour,
> Round the sad walls some scores of churchmen rest,
> Who once laid schemes for honor, wealth and power,
> Drank Whiskey when they could--and tho't it best.
>
> Here long, when evening shed her sober glooms,
> A shatter'd Parson took delight to sleep,
> Or, lost in thought, sat musing o'er the tombs,
> Lamenting there the shepherd and the sheep...

Freneau's experience as a rural teacher among the Long Island Dutch is reflected in "A Characteristic sketch of the LONG ISLAND Dutch:"[8]

Eternal scowerings keep their floors afloat,
Neat as the outside of their Sunday coat;
The wheel, the loom, the female band employ,
These all their pleasure, these their darling joy...

He paid tribute to "Peter Pindar" (English John Wolcot), a popular verse satirist who ridiculed the royalty, in "EPISTLE to PETER PINDAR, ESQ.," whom he called the "happiest wight" ever to write:[9]

We, too, have had your monarch by the nose,
And pull'd the richest jewel from his corwn--
Half Europe's kings are fools, the story goes,
Mere simpletons, and ideots of renown...

He also praised Ben Franklin, recently deceased, in "STANZAS, Occasioned by the Death of Dr. FRANKLIN"--[10]

So long befriended by your art,
Philosopher, we must not part!--
When Monarchs tumble to the ground,
Successors easily are found;

But, matchless FRANKLIN, what a few
Can hope to equal such as YOU,
Who seiz'd from Kings their scepter'd pride,
And tam'd the lightning's darts aside!

Freneau's skepticism about orthodoxy is shown in "Lines Addressed to a dull Country Parson" in four stanzas:[11]

A STEEPLE high and gilded spire,
What more could vanity require?
A silken gown, and varnish'd tub,
   Where twice a week
   You mount to speak,
And give old Satan many a rub...

He added that such sermons, with "pilfer'd scraps from Doctor Blair," do not point to a joyful heaven, but to a "different way."

July 18 to August 10, only one item by Freneau, "On Tobacco," appeared in the *Advertiser*, suggesting a possible illness. The August 10 issue printed "The Removal," about Congress's leaving New York for Philadelphia, republished as "On the Departure of the Grand Sanhedrin," with a sneer at Washington's ornate coach:[12]

From HUDSON'S banks, in proud array,
(Too mean to claim a longer stay)

Their new ideas to improve,
Behold the great SANHEDRIN move!
Such thankless conduct much we fear'd
When Timon's coach stood ready geer'd,
And HE---the foremost on the floor,
Sat, pointing to the Delaware shore...

Freneau also disapproved the snares of easy credit, and wrote "Orator Skip's Apology"--[13]

Most things I bought, but always sigh'd for more--
I bought, indeed---but not one ounce of wit!
Mark that; and mark it down to my confusion--
O credit, credit! What a cheat art thou!...

In the fall of 1790, Freneau wrote few poems. New York must have seemed less attractive without the federal government; and he may have written "The Happy Farmer," a sneer at city life:[14]

From noisy streets of dusty towns
With joy I haste away;
Where lazy Johnnies walk their rounds,
And ladies, with their silken gowns,
Some fading charms display.

Perhaps he was at the point of leaving New York, for he published "Farewell to NEW-YORK"--[15]

NEW-YORK adieu, and may propitious fate
Thy peace extend to time's remotest date...

II. Essays of 1790

Freneau wrote plenty of prose as he grew more critical and political. The Advertiser did not publish regular editorials; but in articles evidently Freneau's, he came more and more to express his views. In 1790, over seventy essays were published in the Advertiser, some in an editorial mood, others comic or satiric, about forty of which appear to be certainly his work.

"A brief account of the Ugly Club"[16] is a comic description of a club probably in Charleston, possibly real; a similar club appears in the Spectator, so that Freneau may have taken the idea from Addison.

"Description of New York one hundred and fifty years hence"[17] predicts a Broadway two and a half miles long and a great international trade. "The OLD SOLDIER and his DOG" is a sentimental piece revealing a cause that Freneau was to make his for many years--government help for the aging veteran:[18]

> ...an old soldier with one arm and a dislocated knee. His former trade was discoverable by a tatter'd uniform...he was followed by a handsome faced dog...
> Friend, said one of our company...Poverty creates a fence around a man incomparably stronger than bars of steel...why then incumber yourself with such an attendant? Name me your price for that dog, and if not beyond the bounds of reason, you shall be paid upon the spot...
> The soldier, at hearing these words, made a halt upon his crutch, and turned full toward us. 'Sir,' said he, addressing himself to the young man, 'it is very true, poverty has no need of guards... But I swear by what was once this arm, and which now lies buried far enough away on the plains of Abraham...that DEATH ONLY shall part me and my dog!

This is typical of Freneau in two ways--sympathy for the wounded soldier and love of animals. He compares the dog with some humans, to the dog's advantage. Certain other essays discuss local problems, like "Hint to the Public" (July 12) on the need for a park, which served as editorials. Freneau used "fillers" for instruction or entertainment, like "Nootka Sound" and "The Great Dismal" in August. "To the Next Congress" satirized congressional motives and puckishly proposed that the body become an "erratic peregrinatious" one and cover the nation like judges:[19]

> Let Fitch build you a steam ship... On this ship erect your Federal Hall, sail up the Chesapeak and the Savannah Sound; visit Sullivan's Island and Charleston, Portsmouth and Boston. Examine the fisheries of the East and the riceries of the South; let molasses and hominy shake hands, and hogoo and johnny cakes kiss...

Now Freneau became keenly interested in the French Revolution, and published "Bastile,"[20] which tells of an elderly prisoner, set free after forty-seven years in the jail, who becomes lost in the busy world outside.

In the fall, he started on an Indian series by "Opay Mico," a chief, with "A short Discourse upon Drunkenness."[21] It is "By OPAY MICO, one of the Indian Kings from the Little Tallassee country, lately departed from this city." A sketch of Alexander McGillivray, leader of those Indians, followed September 9. Other "Indian" essays came along: "Reflections on my Journey from the Tallassee towns to the settlements on the river Hudson," September 8; and "A Discourse upon HORSE SHOES" on September 17. These were to be part of a much longer series by "Tomo Cheeki." But here "Opay Mico" ended his effort for 1790.

In other essays near the end of the year, Freneau wrote on New York's reasons for optimism, on magistrates, patriotism, political letters, printing, the Gulf Stream, Masonry, dancing and balls, Tennessee, Congress, barber poles, public buildings and places, the White Mountains, despotism, Niagara, "great" men, press freedom in England, West Indian creoles, Georgia planters, epic poetry, popery, a proposed theater in New York, the formation of great characters, funeral eulogies, Connecticut (sarcastic), creditors and the funding system (more satire).

Throughout the year, Freneau regarded the city and national issues, Congress, and life generally with amusement. Many of his poems and essays are satirical, even farcical, like "A Discourse upon Barbers' Poles"--[22]

> This spiral circle, Brethren, that twisteth, as it were, about the pole, is, without a doubt, a sort of enigmatical expression, and can be nothing else than a modest hint to him that passeth by, that if the Barber does not now and then bestow some care and labour upon his hair and beard, they will both be tangled and twisted up...

Now and then he took the part of a woman, as in a letter about balls, by one "Henrietta Lively"---[23]

> This morning Betsy Frill came running into our house to communicate an important piece of intelligence. "Bless me, child," says she, "have you heard the news, --The balls are going forward again this season---there's to be a meeting of the young fellows on Wednesday---and I'm told they actually talk of appointing Billy Squib, Jack Rattle, Harry Puff, and Dick Tip, managers..."

But he was serious in discussing patriotism--arguing against it as narrow, and urging world brotherhood--and in essays on Masonry and on the Gulf Stream. Yet he delighted in satire, as in an essay on Congress, and in a comic letter to a young printer or editor:[24]

> Be particularly careful never to insert any of the trivial events that happen in your own county... but if there is a horse-race in England, or in any part of Europe or Asia... copy it totidem verbis... be careful not to forget the muses... If good original poetry cannot easily be had---no matter. The tinsel of the court Poet Malumbrino--the sonorific lines of that painful Epic bard Berodach Baladan, or the gentle somniferous lays of the poetess Morvina... will always furnish out a copious extract for the amusement of those who delight in the works of the muses.

A satire, "On Epic Poetry," a sort of editorial, ridicules epic poets, especially the Connecticut "wits," particularly Timothy Dwight, who had written a long, stiff epic, The Conquest of Canaan. Freneau explained how to create one:[25]

> In the first place borrow, or purchase Pope's Homer's Iliad, the Odyssey, Pitt's or Dryden's translation of Virgil, and if you please, (by way of learning how to avoid the bathos) one of Blackmore's Epics... In the next place look out diligently for a Fable. You might as well make pumpkin pye without pumpkins, or turtle soup from a calf's head... as make an Epic poem without a fable...
>
> If nothing else seems to be proper... turn to the ancient Jewish history (as compiled by Josephus, and others)... There can be no true Epic poem without plenty of butchering work; and here it is displayed to perfection in the annals of the Hebrew butchers... Nonsense is a considerable ingredient... for instance, in describing a battle over-head you may say--"In fields of air unreal hosts contend;" that is to say, there is a battle in the air, fought by nobody...

In December, Freneau got into an amusing controversy over the "wonders of Connecticut," whose boasters he ridiculed. Replying to a skeptic, "D. Doubtful," he "explained" these wonders, citing a squash seed that produced over 200 squashes, a 140-pound pumpkin, a three-headed cabbage, and a twenty-ounce apple; then he added:[26]

> Add to the above wonderful things several wonderful Connecticut women, who have borne, individually, during the last season, from three to four children; all like to do well, and be of good service in their day, either in

> contriving new psalm tunes, writing epic poems, or propagating a fine breed of onions...

Freneau had no love for Yankees in Connecticut, particularly the "wits"--Timothy Dwight, Trumbull, Humphreys, and Barlow--and he enjoyed ridiculing them. A sign of his growing political bias appears in a veiled satire of Hamilton's funding system, by "Consistency," who concludes, "Public creditors! if ye be wise, be quiet where ye are."[27]

III. Last Weeks in the Advertiser, 1791

Planning to establish a newspaper of his own, early in 1791 Freneau was soliciting subscribers when, at the suggestion of Madison, Jefferson offered the journalist a part-time post as translator, at $250 a year. Doubtful of his translating ability, Freneau declined; but Madison continued to urge him to come to Philadelphia.

Meanwhile the poet increased his productivity, doing some three dozen poems, including verse on the veteran, the Negro, the tea drinker, the effects of rum, taxes on newspapers, "court" vogues, city trees, the rural bachelor, the Dutch, and "The Sciota Indian's Complaint," a neglected Indian poem in which the red man protests to the sun, about the Frenchmen and liquor:[28]

> "Thou sun, bright wanderer, ranging o'er these woods,
> Whose ray enlivening sheers Sciota's floods,
> From age to age whose vivid soul endures,
> Whose absence kills me, but whose presence cures...
>
> ...
>
> Once more permit those angry darts to play;
> Kill these NEW MEN, or fright them far away.
>
> "See, Frenchmen mustering by the beat of drum;
> In their whole host are not three quarts of RUM!
> The Britons came with kegs of whiskey strong,
> These with low wines and teas--a feeble throng;
> Hence, strangers, hence..."

This item may have been an indication of Freneau's changing concept of the Indian, evolving in the "Tomo Cheeki" essays of 1795. Also, he had no intention of letting Americans forget the wounded veteran:[29]

Deep in a vale, a stranger new to arms,
Too poor to shine in courts, too proud to beg,
He, who once warr'd on SARATOGA's plains,
Sits musing o'er his fears and wooden leg.

In "Stanzas as Written on the Hills of NEVERSINK, near Sandy Hook, 1790," in some lines he recaptured the wild ecstasy of "The Wild Honey Suckle"--[30]

These heights, the pride of all the coast,
What happy genius plann'd;
Aspiring o'er the distant wave
That sinks the neighbouring land:
These hills for solitude design'd,
This bold and broken shore,
These haunts, impervious to the wind,
Tall oaks, that to the tempest bend,
Half Druid, I adore.

It is an unusual stanza, tetrameter and trimeter, 434343443, nine lines rhyming abcbdedde, an intriguing scheme. Besides using the forms of English poets, Freneau was continually experimenting with variations of his own.

In February he printed a rudely comic poem, "The Jug of Rum," one that might be called his most popular. It reappeared in at least thirty other publications:[31]

Here, only by a cork controul'd,
And slender walls of earthen mould,
In all their pomp of death reside
Revenge, that ne'er was satisfy'd;
The Tree, that bears the deadly fruit
Of murder, maiming, and dispute;
ASSAULT, that innocence assails,
The IMAGES of gloomy jails,
The GIDDY THOUGHT, on mischief bent,
The midnight hour, in folly spent,
ALL THESE within the jug appear,
And JACK, the hangman, in the rear!

Freneau was jealous, yet contemptuous, of David Humphreys, a Connecticut wit, a pompous versifier and pet of Washington who had been appointed a secret agent of the administration in Portugal. Freneau thought him dull, and he probably was:[32]

Whoe'er at court would hope to cut a dash,
He must go loaded with some useful trash;

Something, sage DULLNESS, to assist your reign;
All fancy stuff, all ornament is vain...

"Nothing but useful projects we require,"
(Cries a new-fangled, self-important squire,)
For Lisbon's court has sail'd our man of song:
And trust me, Bards, the MUSES went along:
Since that bright morn he stepp'd on board his brig,
No Muses here--no Muses are with pig...

He added that, were he to pursue Fortune like "Memmius" (Humphreys), he would hurry to court and

Indulge that potent something in the skull,
That makes us famous while it makes us dull...

and again he protested at the "success" of public-figure poets:[33]

Can love of Fame the gentle muse inspire
Where he that hoards the most has all the praise;
Where avarice and her fiends each bosom fire,
All heap the hidden store for rainy days,
  Owning by this perpetual round of toil
  That man was made to grovel on the soil...

Like Jefferson, Freneau approved Paine's Rights of Man--another sign of his increasing interest in politics--and he wrote a poem, "Lines occasioned by reading MR. PAINE's RIGHTS OF MAN."[34]

  Rous'd by the REASON of his manly page,
Once more shall PAINE a listening world engage:
From Reason's source, a bold reform he brings,
In raising up mankind, he pulls down kings,
Who, source of discord, patrons of all wrong,
On blood and murder have been fed too long...

The Rights defended the French Revolution against an attack by Edmund Burke, and supporters of Paine were regarded as dangerous radicals.

Freneau joined a controversy over a municipal law condemning trees, on whether they should be cut down, in "The Landlord's Soliloquy."[35]

  "Thrice happy age, when all was new
And trees untouch'd, unenvied grew,
When yet regardless of the axe,
They fear'd no law, and paid no tax!...
Alas! those times are now forgot,
An iron age is all our lot:

Men are not now what once they were,
To hoard up gold is all their care:
The busy tribe old Plutus calls
To pebbled streets and painted walls;
Trees now to grow, is held a crime,
And THESE must perish in their prime!...

About this time, July, Freneau probably withdrew from editing the Advertiser. He now conferred with Childs and Swaine on founding his Whig paper in Philadelphia, as well as talking to his friends Madison and Henry Lee, who encouraged him to move to the capital. He contributed three poems to the Advertiser: "The Drunkard's Apology" (July 9), "Minerva's Advice" (August 4), and "The Parting Glass" (September 17). And for the New-York Journal of July 16, he wrote a satire on John Adams and Fenno, "POMPOSO and his PRINTER."[36]

Have you a printing press---Pomposo cri'd--
"I have not now"--the gaping Wight repli'd--
But if you'll promise work, I can, with ease,
Provide a press, and play what tune you please."

Getting more involved politically, Freneau apparently joined the essay controversy over Paine's Rights of Man. May 6, the pamphlet began in the Advertiser as a serial, and ran daily till May 27. June 25, John Quincy Adams's "Publicola" essays began, attacking the Rights, Paine, and Jefferson (who had approved it), in eleven numbers, till August 3. On June 28, "Brutus" replied to "Publicola," defending Paine and Jefferson in seven numbers, till July 22. Also "Philodemos" answered John Adams's Davila essays (which had defended aristocracy) in Fenno's Gazette, June 21 to August 12, 1791. Both "Brutus" and "Philodemos" sound very like Freneau.[37] "Philodemos" reviewed history:[38]

> Could we have thought it possible... that within this hundred years, a treatise has been published... containing these very extraordinary positions, viz. That monarchy is the only lawful government...

A week later he continued, quoting Locke:[39]

> Say our opponents, this doctrine founded on equality, may be true a fortiori, but is not true a posteriori. For tho' all men may be equal de jure, they are cer-

> tainly not so de facto...
> On this foundation have De Lolme, and after him our countryman Adams, laboured to establish certain doctrines, which, in my humble opinion, are as fallacious and unsound as they are unfriendly to the rights of mankind, and the dignity of the human character...

"Philodemos" went on to advocate goverment of the people:

> The main drift of Mr. Adams's book is to show us "the utility and necessity of different orders of men, and of an equilibrium of powers and privileges"... The question, then, to be decided... is simply this--is a government compounded of monarchy, aristocracy, and democracy, or in other words, is the English government... the best... ?

He disputed the position that hereditary succession had kept the peace:

> Very far from it! The fact is that the disputes about succession have caused more civil and intestine wars, more bloodshed and misery, in England, than all other causes put together...

Moreover, he said Adams's ideas tended to destroy republicanism:

> Should Mr. Adams's doctrine be well founded, the stupendous fabric which we have lately reared... must soon be "unavoidably" tumbled to pieces...

"Philodemos" dreamed of eventual peace through republican liberty:[40]

> When we see Liberty, after establishing herself in the new world, erecting her standard in one of the largest kingdoms in the old---may we not, with reason, expect that an universal revolution is about to take place---that man in every quarter of the world will finally be completely restored to the rights of his nature; and that the friendly intercourse, which it is the nature of commerce to establish amongst the different nations, will banish from the world that scourge of mankind, War, with all its horrid concomitants--oppression--want, famine, pestilence.

Meanwhile "Brutus" was picking flaws in "Publicola's" arguments, his defense of all things British, his justification of the English Revolution of 1688, and his disparagement of the new France:[41]

> Publicola's letters may be aptly compared to a glittering chain composed of beautiful and highly polished links, hung up on high to dazzle the eyes of the many: But on drawing nigh they discover that it all depends from, and is kept from falling by a miserable rotten thread...

Both series ended before Freneau went to Philadelphia, in mid-August, to call on Jefferson and make arrangements for starting the new paper. His last editorial noted in the Advertiser appeared July 23, a retort to an English poet's "No Abolition of Slavery."

His other 1791 essays included an editorial scolding Pennsylvania for meddling with Congress (January 27); comic talk of a proposal to split the city into wards, by "A Lover of Fun" (January 28); "On Notions," a satire (February 11); a protest at any monopoly of auctions or "vendues" (February 23); Bible inconsistencies, by "Timothy Meanwell" (March 5); a discussion of the benefits of free elections (April 21); an editorial on preserving the city's trees, by "Civis" (May 31); and a complaint about the fining of small tradesmen. None is memorable, yet all are typical topics for a New York editor.

From August on, Freneau's primary interest was his Philadelphia newspaper, the National Gazette.

IV. The National Gazette Years, 1791-1793

In the weeks before the National Gazette appeared, Freneau apparently contributed a few items to his former medium, The Freeman's Journal, including an amusing poem, "An Address to my OLD HAT"--[42]

> Two years acquainted, must we part?
> The very thought afflicts my heart.
> Sheltering my head from sun and storm,
> You kept it either cool, or warm.
> Tho' fashionable folk extol
> The covert of the Parasol,
> To Patriots and Virtue true,
> Still "my old Hat," I stuck to you.
> But now (so Time and Fate decree)
> Alas! you scarcely stick to me...

Another is "An Heroic Tale,"[43] translated from Fontaine (the younger), a tale of the attempt of the French king and queen to leave France. Still another is "An Epistle from PETER PINDAR PENNSYLVANIENSIS, to the Right Honourable WILLIAM PITT, Esq. Chancellor of the Exchequer, &c. in Great Britain," in ten irregular stanzas:[44]

How shall a Western Muse attempt thy praise?
Bold is her wish, but humble are her lays.
Yet since thy genius, which abounds in words,
To admiration ample scope affords,
   My Clio, gentle and sublime,
   Shall celebrate thy worth in rhyme.

And it seems Freneau wrote "VERSES, On the arrival of the PRESIDENT of the United States in Philadelphia, July 6th, 1791," in ten stanzas:[45]

   Green be those laurels, which thou well has won;
Honor's chief prop, and freedom's favorite son;
And as thou still hast grac'd the brave and free,
Friend of the Press, the Press shall honor thee...

Freneau was very busy in September and October, finding a new home, attending to the birth of his first child, and preparing his press for the first issue of the National Gazette, October 31. It was to be his first political venture, and in it he was to be less literary than ever.

Poems in the National Gazette

Yet some new poems did appear in the paper. Freneau took the pseudonym "Sinbat," the name of a sailor, and tried to make the new sheet look creative. But busy as editor, reporter, and writer of news and essays, he had to draw on old poems, and was soon swamped in political controversy. He opened with a "Poetical ADDRESS to the PUBLIC of the UNITED STATES, a gay singsong of five stanzas--[46]

For a share of your favor we aim with the rest--
To enliven the scene we'll exert all our skill;
What we have to impart shall be some of the best,
And Multum in Parvo our text--if you will:
   Since we never admitted a clause in our Creed
   That the greatest employment of life is--to read...

In the first few months of the new paper, new poems included "A Mistake Rectified," by "Sinbat," on the good features of a sailor's life;[47] "The Prudent Philosopher," a comedy on what to do with a burning house;[48] and a serious long poem in six-line pentameter rhymed stanzas, "The Country Printer,"[49] featuring the printer "Type"--

> Abreast the inn--a tree before the door,
> A Printing-Office lifts its humble head,
> Where master Type old journals doth explore
> For news that is thro' all the village read;
> Who, year from year, (so cruel is his lot)
> Is author, pressman, devil--and what not?
>
> ...
>
> Ask you what matter fills his various page?
> A mere farrago 'tis of mingled things;
> Whate'er is done on madam TERRA's stage
> He to the knowledge of his townsmen brings:
> One while, he tells of Monarchs run away;
> And now, of witches drown'd in Buzzard's bay.
>
> Here, full in view, the ink-bespangled press
> Gives to the world its children, with a groan,
> Some born to live a month--a day--some less.
> Some, why they live at all, not clearly known.
> All that are born must die--TYPE well knows that--
> The almanack's his longest-living brat...

The poem is one of Freneau's better long ones. With echoes of Goldsmith's "Deserted Village," it ends on a serious tone of patriotism, the neglected veteran, and the need of printers to distribute knowledge. The "old soldier" was to become a long cause through the first years of the new republic, and Freneau was one of the first to champion him.

As the months wore on, the editor's creative urge in poetry seems to have largely deserted him; he became more and more absorbed in political controversy, and confined himself to prose and satiric verse attacks and replies.

He was stirred by personal abuse and satire in the Echo, a series of comic verse by Federalists in Hartford, to retort in "Receipt to make an ECHO Writer" (March 29, 1792) and "ODE to the ECHO Writer" (April 2); in the latter he apparently assumed that John Trumbull had been the author of the attack:[50]

Bard of the lengthy ode! whose knavish paw
  Ne'er grasp'd the helm, besprent with odious pitch;
'Twas better far, (you know) to practise law,
  Whine at the church or in the court-house screech;
No heart had you to face the wintry blast,
Fight with the storm, or climb the tottering mast.

Meanwhile he had written an editorial poem, untitled, protesting against the placing of Washington's head on the new coins:[51]

Can wits or serious sages say,
Why Congress should refuse that Head
A place upon their coin this day,
O'er which the world hath laurels spread?

Yes; Liberty, celestial Maid
By whom its right to crown was given,
The eager hands of Congress staid;
And claim'd that place, as sent by heav'n...

He expressed sympathy for Holland, recently flooded, in "An ADDRESS to the Citizens of Holland," a short poem:[52]

Columbia's sons would you befriend,
Should you unto their voice attend;
Behold with open arms they stand
Upon the margin of the land,
Proclaiming welcome to these plains,
Where Liberty triumphant reigns...

In another poem he criticized a preacher who milked all cows invading his pasture:[53]

What! did you think your milk of grace would do
For Margaret's brats, that thus you robb'd their cow?...

From May 17 to June 28, 1792, in six installments, he ran a long poem written in 1768. "The Village Merchant," over three hundred lines, all pentameter, mostly heroic couplets, was about the small problems of a small merchant:[54]

  Alack-a-day! on life's uncertain road
How many plagues, what evils must befall;--
Jove has on none unmingled bliss bestow'd,
But disappointment is the lot of all:
Thieves rob our stores, in spite of locks and keys,
Cats steal our cream, and rats infest our cheese,
The gayest coat a grease-spot may assail,
Or Susan pin a dish-clout to its tail. --

Our village merchant (trust me) had his share
Of vile mis-haps---for now, the goods, unpackt,
Discover'd, what might make a deacon swear,
Jugs, cream-pots, and grog-bowls sadly crackt...

On July 4, Freneau published "Independence," a patriotic poem of thirty-two lines in rhymed pentameter:[55]

Remov'd from Europe's feuds, a hateful scene
(Thank heaven, such wastes of ocean roll between)
Where tyrant kings in bloody schemes combine,
And each forebodes in tears, Man is no longer mine...

Something still wrong in every system lurks,
Something imperfect haunts all human works--
War must be hatch'd unthinking men to fleece,
Or we, this day, had been in perfect peace...

Peace to all feuds!--and come the happier day
When Reason's sun shall light us on our way;
When erring man shall all his RIGHTS retrieve,
No despots rule them, and no priests deceive;
'Till then Columbia!--watch each stretch of power
Nor sleep too soundly at the sleeping hour...

Celebrating the birth of the French Revolution, Freneau published "On the Fourteenth of July," in six six-line stanzas, with an unusual rhyme scheme, abcabc, evidence that he still experimented:[56]

BRIGHT DAY, that did to France restore
What priests and kings had seiz'd away,
That bade her generous sons disdain
The fetters that her fathers wore,
The titled slave, a tyrant's sway,
That ne'er shall curse her soil again:

Bright day! a partner in thy joy,
COLUMBIA hails the rising sun;
She feels her toils, her blood repaid,
When fiercely frantic to destroy,
(Proud of the laurels he had won)
The Briton, here, unsheath'd his blade...

Boy! fill the generous goblet high;
Success to France shall be the toast...

Some passing days and rolling years
May see the wrath of kings display'd,
Their wars to prop the tarnish'd crown;
But orphans' groans, and widows' tears,
And justice lifts her shining blade
To bring the tottering bauble down.

Presently the editor wrote a poem to "Crispin O'Connor, Esq. a back woods Planter,"[57] praising his independence, in ten four-line stanzas:

> Prosper your toil!--but, friend, had you remain'd
> In lands, where stars and garter'd nobles shine,
> When you had thus, to sixty years attain'd,
> What different fate, 'Squire Crispin, had been thine!

Freneau's calm was now broken by an attack in Fenno's paper, by Hamilton as "T. L.", accusing him of taking a government salary as a bribe for collusion with Jefferson in the National Gazette. He struck back at his rival editor:[58]

> Since the day we attempted the NATION'S GAZETTE
> Pomposo's dull printer does nothing but fret...

And, retorting to Federalist enemies, he wrote "To the National Gazette"--[59]

> For nine months past, a host of busy foes
> Have buzz'd about your nose,
> White, black, and grey,
> By night and day;
> Garbling, lying,
> Singing, sighing:--
> These eastern gales a cloud of insects bring
> That flattering, snivelling, whispering on the wing,
> And wafted still as Discord's demon guides,
> Flock round the flame, that yet must scorch their hides...

Now, realizing that the continuing charges were written by Hamilton, Freneau published an affidavit of denial. Then he ridiculed the aristocrats' fancy carriages in "A Curious Dialoge,"[60] probably with Washington's handsome vehicle in mind. But the papers were filled with letters arguing pro and con for Hamilton or Jefferson, so it was over two weeks before Freneau broke into verse again, to rebuke his assailants, in "An Old Heathen Story," of the Greek Aristippus scolding a "set of whelps."[61]

> "Home to your straw!--such contests I disdain.--
> Learn this,
> ('Tis not amiss)
> For men
> I keep a pen,
> For dogs--a cane."

Three weeks later he ridiculed speculators, especially Federalists, in "The Speculator,"[62] evidently with William Duer in mind. Duer, former assistant secretary of the Treasury, was a leader of New York speculation, and now in jail:

> Three weeks, and more, thus pass'd in airs of state,
> The fourth beheld the mighty bubble fail--
> And he, who countless millions own'd so late
> Stopt short---and clos'd his triumphs in a JAIL.

Replying to a critic who said he ridiculed religion, Freneau wrote:[63]

> If of Religion I have made a sport
> Then why not cite me to the Bishops court?--
> Fair to the world let every page be set
> And prove your charge from National Gazette...

Three days later he offered another poem, on a favorite subject, "Advice to Ladies not to Neglect the Dentist."[64]

Now the editor was swamped by letters for and against Hamilton, with Hamilton himself writing letters to discredit Freneau and Jefferson. There was little time or mood for verse in over two months and then only in crude humor. Commenting on the Liberty bust, moved out of Congress Hall, pretending the contribution was "from correspondents"--a then often used veil for editors--Freneau printed this:[65]

> WHAT, --not content with pulling down
> Fair LIBERTY from her exalted station,
> Our Congress such contempt have shewn
> For HER, the guardian Goddess of the nation,
> They've thrust her where, with foul dishonor,
> They mean t'insult--and p---- upon her!

Soon he translated a poem to Americans, by the French Patriotic Society of Charleston,[66] and published another, "The Pyramid of the Fifteen American States."[67] These were followed by "Present Views of France and her Combined Enemies," a poem of sympathy for the French king and queen, condemning the new despots of Europe--the closing lines of the ninth and final stanza:[68]

> O FRANCE! the world to thee must owe
> A debt they ne'r can pay:
> The RIGHTS OF MAN you bid them know,

And kindle REASON'S DAY!
COLUMBIA, in your friendship blest,
Your gallant deeds shall hail--
On the same ground our fortunes rest,
Must flourish, or must fail...
Defeat would all their arms disgrace,
AND LIBERTY PREVAIL!

Freneau wrote many short pieces of verse like "Short Canes!" (January 12, 1793) and an item about a shad (February 2), that are often comic, usually political. Now the new fad for balloons attracted him. Blanchard, a Frenchman, was demonstrating them, and Freneau wrote a seven-stanza poem to him, with advice:[69]

Yet, travelling thro' the azure road,
Soar not too high for REASON'S ken;
Reflect, our humble safe abode
Is all that NATURE meant for men:
   Take in your sails before you freeze
   And sink again among the trees.--

Now absorbed in politics, the editor published no poetry till May--"A New Song," in seven stanzas, first in the New York Journal, on the rights of man:[70]

God save the Rights of Man!
Give us the heart to scan
Blessings so dear:
Let them be spread around
Wherever man is found,
And with the welcome sound
Ravish his ear.

He translated the poem of Pichon, "Ode to Liberty," of twelve stanzas:[71]

Thou splendid light, that clouds obscur'd
   So long from Gallic lands,
Goddess, in ancient days ador'd
   By Gallia's conquering bands:
Thou LIBERTY! whom savage kings
Have plac'd among forbidden things,
Tho' still averse that man be free,
Secret, they bow to Liberty...

Over a month later, Freneau published his "REFLECTIONS on the death of a Country PRINTER," in four stanzas:[72]

Like Sybils' leaves, his sheets he spread
To keep in awe the well born few:
Stock-jobbers fainted while they read--
Each hidden scheme expos'd to view--
Who could such doctrines spread abroad
So long--and not be clapper claw'd?

...

What shall be done in such a case?--
Shall I, because one brother fails,
Call in his bull-dogs from the chace
To loll their tongues, and drop their tails?
No faith!--th'aristocratic crew
No longer fly--than we pursue.--

This poem, it seems, was Freneau's way of justifying his attacks on opponents. Two weeks later he published "Patriotic Stanzas on the Anniversary of the Storming of Bastille."[73]

To Gallia's rich and splendid crown,
This mighty Day gave such a blow
As Time's recording hand shall own
No former age had power to do:
No single gem some Brutus stole,
But instant ruin seiz'd the whole...

And there were brief political retorts: "On a late memorable naval engagement,"[74] twelve eight-line stanzas on the battle between the French L'Embuscade (Captain Bompard) and the British Boston (Captain Courtney), a French victory; and "Orlando's Flight," a comic poem, satirized the Philadelphia doctors who fled from the yellow fever:[75]

'Twas right to fly! for well I wean
In Stygian worlds, by Jove's decree,
No blushing bosom e'er was seen,
Or running brook, or budding tree:
No splendid meats, no flowing bowls
Smile o'er the meagre feast of souls...

A fortnight later came "Elegy on the Death of a Blacksmith," in seven ballad-like stanzas, semi-comic:[76]

He blew up no coals of sedition, but still
His bellows was always in blast;
And I will acknowledge (deny it who will)
That one Vice, and but one, he possess'd.

No actor was he, or concern'd with the stage,
No audience, to awe him, appear'd;

Yet oft in his shop (like a crowd in a rage)
The voice of a hissing was heard...

A week later the editor printed "Lines Addressed to a very little Man, who was fond of walking with a very large Cane," comic verse in seven four-line irregular stanzas:[77]

Who bade you bear this huge Cyclopean beam,
Yourself an insect at its foot,
Which, if it fell, would end your mortal dream,
And put your daylight out!

Perhaps Freneau, caught in the midst of an epidemic, was doing what he could to cheer up his readers. Presently he published "Quintilian to Lycidas" in four six-line stanzas--another example of his habit of experimenting with patterns:[78]

Stay not too close in learning's shop;--
'Till time a riper mind prepares,
The ball, the marble, and the top
Are books that should divide your cares--
The lads that life's gay morn enjoy,
I'm pleas'd to see them act the boy...

In short, the author was saying be yourself!

Freneau wrote no more new verse in 1793. All summer he had been blamed by Federalists for the witty satires of the "Probationary Odes," by "Jonathan Pindar," of the "Feds." But they were the work of St. George Tucker, a Virginia judge. Here is a sample, as he introduced himself to government officials as an office seeker:[79]

So please your Worships, Honors, LORDSHIPS, GRACES!
I JONATHAN to PETER PINDAR cousin,
Hearing that you possess a mint of places,
Have come to ask for less than half a dozen...

The failure of the National Gazette--which expired on October 26, 1793--probably affected Freneau deeply. It had been his most intense journalistic experience. The heated controversies of 1792-1793 were not conducive to his best creative work, so it is not surprising that he wrote little verse or that what he did write is hardly memorable.

V. Essays in the National Gazette

As might be expected of a Whig newspaper absorbed in controversy with the conservative Gazette of the United States, the Federalists, Hamilton, and the federal administration, most of the prose in the National Gazette, besides the news, was far from literary. Yet there was a vast amount of prose, and most apparently by the editor--editorials, descriptions, and heated "contributions" arguing for democracy, the common man and France, and against aristocracy, monarchy, Britain, the Hamilton issues and the conservatism of the wealthy. In 1792, a split begun by Hamilton's attacks on Freneau and Jefferson resulted in a division of voters into two parties--the Federalists led by Hamilton and the Republicans (later, Democrats) led by Jefferson. In 1792 and 1793, the National Gazette was the voice of the new Democracy.

Very few of the essays evidently by Freneau have been collected; so ascriptions must, in most cases, depend on style, ideas, or content resembling the editor's personality or experience. As he apparently used over 300 pseudonyms, these also serve as guides. In such ascriptions, Leary has taken an ultra-conservative view, crediting Freneau only with items certainly his. Such a view omits a large percentage of the items probably his. The present writer, having long made a study of the prose, feels impelled to assign these as "probably" by Freneau.

Prose written under the stress of attack and retort can hardly be literary; the essays, therefore, have little or no value except as examples of the issues of the day. So we must hunt for the items relatively free from them, for "literature." One such is an early editorial--"The interest of the Northern and Southern States forever inseparable:"[80]

> It seems to have been the design of nature in her formation and distribution of that part of North America, known by the name of the United States, that a mutual dependence should take place between the northern and southern inhabitants. The New-England states, naturally narrow, and their lands in general not very fertile or productive, will ever be under the necessity of keeping a vast number of their people on the watry element; of this number the fisheries will occupy a considerable share. The ex-

> portation of the manufactures and commodities of those four states will engage another part; but a large surplus must in a short time, I may even say, would be absolutely out of employ at this instant, were it not for the carrying trade of the southern states...

In January, 1792, Freneau first published an article on the Indian's rights, a dream essay in which a wooden head on a ship's bow orates:[81]

> "I have every reason to believe, gentlemen, that I was placed here as the emblem of valour, activity, perseverance, industry and cunning. So far, therefore, have your countrymen testified in favor of an opinion, almost universally exploded, that the inhabitants of the western forests have some affinity with the human species. I wish they had gone a little farther, and in their general conduct towards our tribes in peace and war treated us as beings possessed of reason, and practicing some few of the inferior virtues. Alas, it is too evident from their actions, that they place us on a footing with the beasts of the wilderness, and consider an Indian and a Buffaloe as alike entitled by nature to property or possession.
>
> "My heart bleeds within me when I reflect upon the wrongs of my countrymen, the insignificant rank they appear to hold in the scale of animated being, and their probable extirpation from the continent of America..."

This essay typifies Freneau's early romantic conception of the red men as an abused, yet ideal symbol of the primitive, pure way of life. Years later, he was apparently to change to a practical, realistic attitude.

An item indicating his habit of observing people and places, an introduction to "The Jug of Rum," is "On Country Taverns:"[82]

> A country Tavern is generally a place of rendezvous for all the choice spirits of a neighborhood. Here petty law suits are decided at least once a fortnight, and he must be an indifferent justice of the peace, who presides at such trials (as they are called) who will not drink both with plaintiff and defendant, after the suit is decided...
>
> Happy would it be for every community if ardent spirits could be banished from amongst them...

"On the Origin of Nobility" is an example of the philosophy behind Freneau's hatred of monarchy and wealth, evidently an editorial:[83]

> There being...different grades of virtue in the human species...it would seem proper enough that the most virtuous should be the real nobility... Unfortunately, virtue proved to be not hereditary; and when men were once induced to count upon a parental transmission of the virtues...they soon experienced the fatal consequences... Hence, the idea of virtue itself became changed...among the Romans, in particular, for many ages, the word imported nothing more than courage or brutal ferocity...
>
> ...Most of the present real nobility in Europe, as well as Asia, may be called the posterity of invaders and plunderers... the peasantry ...are no other than vassals to the heirs of plundered property...

A few days later the editor reviewed a book about Western America by one Mr. Stuart, "said to be in the employ of the British court," who had spent four years travelling in the Far West, finding several Indian nations superior to those in the East, living in "a state of society not far removed from the European,"[84] doubtless an exaggeration; yet the romantic Freneau seemed willing to accept it.

"Hatteras Shoals" is the sort of description that Sailor Freneau would write from first-hand experience:[85]

> At the time of Sir Walter Raleigh's approaching the American shores, the shoals in the vicinity of Hatteras were found to be extremely dangerous, and no vessels, in that latitude, ventured within seven leagues of the land. From a survey of the ancient drafts of this part of the coast, there can be no doubt but the fears of former navigators were not without foundation, as these shoals are laid down very large in extent, and in many places covered not with more than five or six feet water...
>
> At present the out-shoals, which lie about fourteen miles south-east of the Cape, are but of five or six acres' extent... On the shoalest part of these is, at low water, about ten feet, and here at times the ocean breaks in a tremendous manner...
>
> ...A little north of the Cape is good anchorage in four or five fathoms, and, with the wind to the westward, a boat may land in safety, and even bring off casks of fresh water, plenty of which is to be found every where on the beach...

At this time, the editor chose to remind Philadelphians of the value of their shade trees, in the essay "On Trees in Cities:"[86]

> A citizen may be termed an artificial being, as both his residence and means of life are the peculiar effect of art...
>
> A city, then, being the constrained residence of so many thousands of men, what wonder that they have not, generally, taken more pains to transplant the imitative works of nature (such as a row of fine trees)...
>
> Legislatures and city corporations have ever been inimical to trees in cities.--About nine years ago the attempt was made in Philadelphia to cut down all the trees--the public, however, demurred to the decree, which, together with Mr. Hopkinson's Columnal Orator, saved the lives of these useful and amusing companions.--[87]
>
> ...Trees in towns are conducive to health as well as convenience; they please the eye, obstruct the burning rays of the summer sun, and impart, in some degree, the blessings of rural life to him who is confined to the counter, the shop-board, and other sedentary employments in a large city.

The editor followed with his poem on the subject, from the Advertiser, "The Landlord's Soliloquy."[88]

"Above-Board," evidently Freneau in disguise, now gaily rebuked the Senate for keeping its doors closed:[89]

> Has the Almighty pledged himself to distinguish America with such peculiar favor, that the Federal Dome shall for ever continue inaccessible to corruption? Has he promised, that whenever a man, subject to the common frailties of humanity, presents himself as candidate for a seat, the fiery ordeal of electioneering shall completely melt away and consume all the alloy of vice and folly, and leave him nought but sterling virtue to carry into Congress?
>
> Were the millennium soon to commence, we might rest secure. But the present Congress themselves have already sounded the alarm: they have told us that, by an encrease in the representation, the avenues of the House will be widened for the admission of improper characters. And if, at the next election, even one unprincipled individual clambers into Congress, he alone can, by newspaper complaints of misrepresentation, so persecute the short-hand-writers, as either to silence them altogether, or to make them glad, for peace's sake, to submit their manuscripts to his inspection,--to receive from his hands whatever he thinks proper to write...
>
> Were there no other mode of preventing the baneful effects of such a dangerous control over the liberty of the press, it would be wise in the State Legislatures, instead

> of laboring to unlock the doors of the Senate, rather to aim at locking up those of the House of Representatives, whilst that body is yet pure and uncontaminated, --and breaking the key, lest they should ever be opened again...

Now, before he had become involved in bitter political disputes, Freneau was at his satiric best. Soon after, as "Magnet," he pled with tongue in cheek for a plan of "Universal Peace:"[90]

> A citizen of the United States proposes a convention of nations for forming a constitution, to put this project into execution, having certainly discovered that the surface of this globe is subject to perpetual and periodical changes, and that above two millions of acres annually emerge from the ocean in some places, while the same quantity is overwhelmed in others by magnetic tides. --These principles are now pretty well known in America and Europe... Were these United States subject to a monarch, by the laws of nature and of nations these new-discovered lands might become his property...
>
> ...the present plan is, that all national disputes may be settled by law, and that the two millions of acres annually may be appropriated as a fund to defray the expense of the universal government... Suppose these new lands not to be sold but rented... at the rate of one dollar per acre per annum... put out to use at the lawful interest of six per cent... in time all the land would become public property...

As partisan politics engulfed him, Freneau lost most of his impartiality and became a passionate disputant in such essays as: "Sentiments of a Republican,"[91] against the funding system; on the two main parties and opposing a large public debt;[92] on Federalist fallacies;[93] a satire on Congress, "Useful Animadversions;"[94] an angry retort to Fenno's Gazette of the United States,[95] etc. Essays with no coloring of contemporary politics became harder to find in the National Gazette.

Early in May, the National Gazette carried a long comic satire on aristocrats and speculators, "Plan for a Nobility in the United States,"[96] from the American Daily Advertiser, but probably by Freneau, suggesting that the Treasury give to all speculators who had $150,000 to $600,000 a bonus of $150,000 more, with titles like "the order of the Leech" or "Their Rapacities," etc., and base the nobility on the funded debt. (At this time a fury of speculation in government certificates in New York had collapsed.) This was a slap at Federalists, Hamilton, and speculation.

"Theatre" was an editorial for a republican stage, one not devoted to the glorification of royalty and tyrants, an idea typical of Freneau:[97]

> It has frequently been the misfortune of theatrical exhibitions to be ranked amongst the frivolous and dissipated amusements cultivated and patronized by the great, in despotic or aristocratic governments, where the people are amused by the policy of the rulers to prevent them from looking into the rights of man. A discrimination ought, however, in justice to be made between theatrical exhibitions and others of a meaner or really mischievous nature. A virtuous people will always insure a chaste theatre, and no manager would dare to permit loose or indecent dramatic performances on the American stage, if he had reason to think his audience were disinclined to be entertained with productions of that sort... The first duty of the stage ought to be, to inculcate honesty, patriotism, morality, and good will to mankind, instead of that savage heroism of restless tyrants...

Stage plays about royalty were popular all through the eighteenth and nineteenth centuries, and Freneau's was one of the few voices raised against them.

Freneau was fond of writing comic "rules"--and because of its similarity to Franklin's satire on Britain, "Rules by Which a Great Empire May Be Reduced to a Small One," a new satire on the Federalists, "Rules for Changing a Limited Republican Government into an Unlimited Hereditary One," evidently by Freneau, is worth quoting:[98]

> I. It being necessary, in order to effect the change, to get rid of constitutional shackles, and popular prejudices, all possible means and occasions are to be used for both these purposes.
>
> II. Nothing being more likely to prepare the vulgar mind for aristocratical ranks and hereditary powers, than TITLES, endeavor in the offset of the government to confer those on its most dignified officers. If the principal magistrate should happen to be particularly venerable in the eyes of the people, take advantage of that fortunate circumstance in setting the example...
>
> VI. But the grand nostrum will be a PUBLIC DEBT, provided enough of it can be got, and it be medicated with the proper ingredients... Assume all the debts of your

> neighbours... get as much debt as can be raked and scraped together...

Freneau's longtime impatience with orthodoxy is expressed in an October editorial, using a story to illustrate a point:[99]

> There is a description of people, more or less abounding in every state, who view the Constitution of the United States through such a peculiar medium of vision as to discover not a particle of spot or blemish in the whole... This would be well enough and no one would blame them ... were it not that every one shall see in the same manner, although perhaps not looking through the same glass with themselves.
>
> In some states a man is not reckoned a good patriot, or at all gifted with civil orthodoxy, unless, previous to receiving any public appointments, he submits to the obligations of a religious test; as much as to say, Think in all respects as we do, even in the most indifferent matters, or we will not be bound to suppose that you are capable or worthy... The puny effects of certain scheming gentlemen, to depreciate the character of the National Gazette, because it does not in every column hold up to the people absolute perfection in the measures of government, as well as in the government itself, puts me in mind of a passage in Nicholas Klimius's Subterranean Journey...

On current controversies among teachers at the local college of medicine, evidently the editor did a gay satire signed "Peter Plagiary," recommending the borrowing of lectures from famous authors:[100]

> Odds boddikins!!... why all this pother concerning the medical lectures of late? Why not save the students of medicine the trouble of travelling three or four hundred miles, especially when it can be done at once, by a single stroke of the pen?
>
> In turning over the old newspapers of this state, I have frequently seen receipts to make epic poems, receipts to write antifederal essays; but I do not recollect ever to have read a receipt to compose a course of medical lectures... I have ... tossed up the following...
>
> RECIPE.
>
> 1st. If from an ignorance of the English grammar, a certain muddiness of the understanding... you are not able to compose an introductory lecture, a few pages on the importance of health, transcribed verbatim from Sir William Temple's essay on health and long life, will answer the most sanguine expectations...

> 2d. As the theory of fevers will employ a large portion of your time, and as it would be unfashionable to detail the whims of Dr. Boerhave, and for the sake of variety, it would be improper to copy from the printed edition of Dr. Cullen, you may retail the twelve manuscript lectures of this celebrated professor...

Freneau's humanitarian attitude toward Indians is reflected in an editorial "On the Indian War"--[101]

> To extirpate the Indians, as it would be inhumane, so it would be without benefit to us; and as to compelling them to an honourable peace, little is to be expected from a treaty dictated by force... it is hopeless... for what armaments can penetrate regions comparatively unknown, to pursue an enemy that flees as you advance... ?...
>
> If this war continues, it is easy to say its expenditures will be growing... a regular and growing drain upon the treasury... to say nothing of the discouragement it affords to Europeans to come into this country... Let it be the study then of the people, in their elections, to choose those men to represent them that may lay the axe at the root of this evil... thus the poor Indian may become safe in the hunting grounds allotted to him; and the country enjoy a dignity, credit and peace proportionate to the wisdom and integrity of its views.

Early in November the National Gazette carried a series of paragraphs as "reflections," editorials typical of Freneau in all his newspapers despite the mask, "Detached reflections from a correspondent:"[102]

> 1. A speculating spirit, if prevalent, is always dangerous... more particularly so when it infects the government itself. In that case the people and their interests are at the mercy of those whose situation and information enable them to take undue advantage of unsuspecting ignorance...
>
> 2. With some characters every matter relating to government must be rendered mysterious, as if on purpose to bewilder the enquirer... This is something like the glorious uncertainty of the law, which has been the support of thousands in all ages who must have turned to some less lucrative employment, had the code of legislation been disgraced with plain expression and the open simplicity of honesty and common sense...

Another of Sailor Freneau's descriptions apparently taken from personal observations is the essay "Cat-Island:"[103]

> This island, one of the Bahamas, is remarkable as being the first land on which Columbus set foot in America, and where, for the first time, the nations of two distant parts of the globe were introduced to each other. Cat-Island, called by the ancient native Indians GUANIHANI, lies between the twenty-fourth and twenty-fifth degrees of north latitude, and in about the 76th degree of western longitude from the meridian of London. Such travellers as visit Providence, frequently take a trip from thence to Cat-Island, ninety miles distant...
>
> Cat-Island is long, and generally narrow, the most easterly of the northern Bahamas, and lies clear of the Bahama Bank. In length it is about forty-three miles, seven in breadth on an average, and extends from north to south. The shores are in most parts faced with reefs of sharp rocks lying about half a mile, frequently less, from the land, and on the western side extending to a much greater distance. Between these reefs and within them there is good anchorage on a sandy bottom, and the landing is not very difficult, particularly on the western shore; except there has recently been strong northwesterly gales...
>
> The first discovery of Guanihani could not have inspired very elevated hopes in the crew of Columbus. The soil is generally barren, being a loose dry sand covered with small woods, in some places almost impenetrable, and infested with millions of lizards, some guanas, and several species of land-crabs, which, with a few goats and wild hogs, might have been justly denominated the lords and sole possessors of the soil till the pirates, and latterly some settlers from Providence, planted themselves on these barren shores...

The writer adds that, "from an attentive inspection some years ago," he found salt ponds and ruins of buildings, probably forts, and learned that the fishing and the "turtling" were good.

Now, while writing articles attacking John Adams and praising George Clinton (governor of New York), candidates for Vice-President, the editor, apparently as "Artist," argued for a patent system financing inventors, in "A Suggestion."[104] And in "Sketch of the present situation of Vermont,"[105] he praised the "abilities, enterprise and industry" of Vermonters, still joined to New Hampshire.

"To the Noblesse and Courtiers of the United States" is an ironic protest at the "royal" features of the administration, including the President's behavior at receptions and the plans to celebrate his birthday, as imitating England:[106]

> Wanted against the 21st of February, a person who is well skilled in the trade of versifying, and who is willing to offer up his talents to government as a Poet Laureat. As this is somewhat of a new trade in the United States, and the person offering himself may be awkward in the duties which he is called to perform, it is intended to write to the poet laureat of his Britannic majesty for a few lessons. One thing, however, will be certainly required, a dexterity in composing birth-day odes, soaring above this clod for models for the characters laureated. To compare an officer of government to any thing on this earth, would be an anti-hyperbole, unsuited to the majesty of the subject... To give a more perfect accommodation to this almost new appointment, certain monarchical prettinesses must be highly extolled, such as levees, drawing-rooms, stately nods instead of shaking hands, titles of office, seclusion from people, &c....

After comments on balloons, Boston aristocracy, Connecticut monarchism, the danger of idolizing Washington, the criminal law code (too severe), the non-payment of Frenchmen who served in the Revolution, titles, the growth of American republicanism, closed Senate doors, King Louis XIV, the editor published a discussion of the American theater, then much in the talk of the day:[107]

> A Theatre is now erected in Charleston, S. C. in consequence of a repeal of a former prohibitory law... and we hear strenuous exertions are shortly to be made in Boston for a like repeal... Under judicious management, there is no doubt but a theatre might be morally instructive and innocently entertaining... at the same time it is too true that many plays, now in high vogue, ought to undergo a sentence of expulsion, as illy adapted to inculcate that virtuous simplicity, humility of demeanor and love of equal liberty which ought alike to actuate governors and governed in a pure and virtuous republic. If... we are to be entertained with dramatic productions exhibiting the theatrical foppery of fretful, passionate kings, pouting queens, rakish princes and flirting princesses, knavish ministers and peevish secretaries, lamenting misfortunes in which the bulk of mankind are in no way concerned... better that we were without them... Few stage exhibitions can, indeed, be useful in any degree, except such as inculcate an observance of the moral and social duties, or in some shape tend to better the heart, without vitiating the understanding by an overstrained address to the fancy...

Another "reflections" editorial[108] presently talked about "men of exorbitant ambition," geniuses, dangerous ministers free to act, self-important officials, etc. As "A Republican,"[109] it was probably the editor who justified the execution of Louis XVI, whose life "ought to be considered but as the life of one man," and who had shown himself "a traitor to his country." Then, retorting to a writer who had said that, in France, an aristocrat was hated worse than an atheist, it was evidently Freneau who declared the aristocrat was more dangerous:[110]

> The Aristocrat oppresses the moral and physical faculties of man; the Deist, or Atheist, oppress no body.---His opinions are his own, and ask not the aid of rich and cruel priests; he erects no piles, stakes, nor fires, nor kindles the destructive animosity of religious warfare...
>
> And let us enquire also, what can be the creed of crafty and covetous priests, who sacrifice every consideration to their thirst for gold?---how can they have the assurance to profess the christian religion---a religion which inculcates poverty, humility, forgiveness of injuries, and even love towards our enemies!
>
> The truth is, they find it their interest to prevent light from spreading among mankind. They are sensible that true science, in restoring the rights of human nature, would soon convince men that they can be happy without the intervention of crowned or religious despots...

Throughout early 1793, Republicans in Congress tried desperately to oust Hamilton from the Treasury. But his replies to attacks cleared him from charges of mismanagement. When Congress voted him vindicated (by a Federalist majority), Freneau, with others, strove mightily to prove him guilty despite this vote---Freneau evidently as "Timon" in long addresses "To the Freemen of the United States."[111]

But soon the editor was diverted by a rising interest in France and its new ambassador, Genet, over whom he became too enthusiastic. As "The Spirit of MDCCLXXVI," it was doubtless he who defended France and blasted Britain:[112]

> The mercury of republicanism in this city seems to rise and fall with the good or bad fortune of France, and her measures are approved or condemned according to her victories or defeats... Some Englishmen among us... forget that they are in the republic of America; they for-

> get that Great-Britain was the enemy of this country and endeavoured to enslave us... Are not Frenchmen asserting the same natural rights which we claimed...?... Who burned your towns, laid waste your country, and rioted upon your miseries?

In the same issue, Freneau replied to England's Fox, who had said that war was man's natural passion, with a rather Shaftesburian philosophy:

> Mr. Fox intimates... that War is the natural passion of men, and (he feared) would always continue to be so.---It may well be questioned, however, whether this propensity is not rather artificial than natural, and introduced thro' the vice of governments rather than instilled into the human constitution thro' the immediate design of the creator... The very virtues of monarchy have all a cruel and sanguinary tendency... Monarchy originated in murder, violence and robbery... man is naturally good, but... his species has been vitiated and debased by preposterous modes of government...

With these items--with Congress adjourned and contributors mostly gone home--the editor was evidently writing almost the whole paper. An essay by "An Old Soldier," a favorite pseudonym with him, the first of scores apparently by him, now appeared. He upbraided critics of France and attacked Britain, perhaps in order to influence the President, who soon declared a Proclamation of Neutrality in the Franco-English War. Days later, evidently as "A Freeman,"[113] Freneau urged a warm welcome for Genet, about to arrive. This impetuous Frenchman was received enthusiastically by the general public, but very coolly by the President.

Presently, as "Y.," reviewing a book, Brissot's Nouveau Voyage dans les Etats Unis (1788), the editor said, defending Joseph Reed (once president of Pennsylvania) against a charge of cruelty to the Quakers:[114]

> A Frenchman, of some eminence, has his mind poisoned in private conversation, by the most injurious and palpable falsehoods, which, on his return to France, he publishes... as to Mr. REED---that martyr to secret calumny---it is shameful that his character should be still persecuted by the same lying spirit... these two men [Quakers] were executed on the 4th day of November 1778... he did not take his seat, as a member of the council, till the 24th of November... he had never given

> any orders on the occasion [becoming president], nor had he any authority to give orders for the execution of any man, or to vote... till some time after...

After more articles defending France, and after Genet's arrival, it seems that the "Old Soldier" offended Washington by sneering at his proclamation and his aristocratic behavior.[115] Then evidently, the editor wrote a long epitaph on neglected veterans; this was a favorite form with Freneau, and was preceded by a "dream" --[116]

> Ruminating the other evening, over the prominent features of the late war... I arrived at the period when the army was disbanded. I reflected on the injustice that ensued to the war-worn veteran... I compared the merits of the soldier and the citizen creditor... with those of the speculating swarm, who became...possessed of the property of the former. "Alas!" said I to myself, "cruel has been the lot of the American patriots..." Nature gave way---a languor pervaded my frame; and I sunk into a slumber on my chair. I found myself on the post road, between Philadelphia and New York. By the road side, there stood a rude, but striking monument... The inscription was cut in Roman capitals. I read it---and awoke, with emotions I cannot describe!

THE INSCRIPTION

STOP, Traveller!
And
View this TOMB:
It covers the Trunk
of
A VALIANT SOLDIER!
Among the first in that glorious struggle for
Liberty, which gave to his
country Independence;
He fought her battles.---
He lived to see HER free;
HIMSELF--maimed, miserable, dependent!

Amid political disputes, Freneau wrote an editorial on the moon, with some errors recognizable after 170 years:[117]

> Of all the astronomers, Mr. Herschel has been the most successful in bringing us to an intimate acquaintance with our attendant planet, the Moon. He has totally exploded the old opinion of there being no air, by his discovery of three burning mountains, or volcanoes, on different parts of the Moon's surface, which could not exist without air... It has long been my opinion, that the luminous portions... are seas, and the dark parts land; and, to the

> lunarians, the seas and lands of this earth, no doubt, exhibit an appearance greatly similar... If this earth, which is thirteen times larger, and superior in every respect, exhibits such wretched scenes of blood, misery, and desolation, as we daily see or hear of, the moon, being no other than her kitchen, is by fair inference a world of war and vengeance, without the least interval of pacification, & the menials that inhabit her are undoubtedly a set of blackguards.

It appears that all summer Freneau filled most of his paper with criticisms of the foreign policy and with defenses of France, under various pen names: "Old Soldier," "Citizen of the United States," "A Friend to Peace and Mankind," "Observator," "Philadelphus," "Brother-Tory," "An American," "Timon," "Juba," etc.; and naturally he editorialized on the Declaration of Independence:[118]

> Tomorrow completes SEVENTEEN years since the Declaration of Independence in this country. By accounts from different parts of the United States, the day will be very generally celebrated, in commemoration of that extraordinary event, which gave birth to the infant liberties of 3 millions (at this day near 4 millions) of our countrymen, and which seems finally to involve in its consequences a new political order and condition of things among mankind, infinitely more favourable than at any former period, to the general happiness... Let republican patriotism revive, then, and let every individual reacknowledge those great and benign principles that actuated his countrymen or himself on the FOURTH OF JULY, 1776, in the glorious cause of the rights of human nature, political equality, and a government founded on the authority of the people.

Presently there followed an amusing letter about a balloonist, one Decker, and the burning of his balloon in 1789:[119]

> Everyone remembers the <u>celebrated</u> Balloon for which the late Mr. DECKER set a subscription on foot in New York, in January 1789. The subscription was filled by the July following, and the day fixed for the ascent of the adventurous aeronaut. It is almost needless to bring into view the fate of that immense unwieldy smoke-bag. It was attempted to be filled by means of a fire being set to... damp straw, chopped wood, &c. &c. but... it was never completely inflated... the balloon... took fire, and it was with some difficulty the aeronaut escaped from the conflagration with the loss of his whiskers... A few days before Mr. Decker's intended ascent, the following address was sent...

> Your visit to America is pleasing to every one...I have read...many publications of the surprizing and successful voyages...into the upper regions...I am half tempted to request a passage... we are informed, that the upper regions belong solely to a great prince... so that should he happen to be a little out of humour on the day of your ascension, &...should chance to meet you, full butt, and demand to see your pass... Alas! I fear nothing less than the entire annihilation of Mr. Decker, balloon and all, in an instant!...therefore pray take my advice, and arm your balloon with one of Dr. Franklin's specific conducting rods... then will Mr. Decker and I, if permitted, triumphantly soar aloft, and dare to look his godship full in the face, undaunted at his grim, surly phiz and terrific appearance, and exultingly proceed on in spite of all his feeble efforts to prevent us...!

This is a fair example of Freneau's kind of humor, though less appealing now than in 1793. He also resented the assumed superiority of aristocrats, as in an essay by "L.," one of his pseudonyms:[120]

> I find an opinion is endeavoured to be propagated by the advocates of aristocracy in this country, that public affairs should only be discussed by "men of property," or what with them is a synonymous term, "reputation."
>
> Strange, that certain insects who have been thawed into existence by the sunshine of the army dues, and owe their whole consequence to the easy credulity of a defrauded public, should assume thus much over what is the birth-right of every free American, the right of freely discussing public measures... Forget not, gentlemen aristocrats, that ten or fifteen years ago, nay, but three or four with some of you, you would have been difficulted to make out _twa dips to a baubee_; and that altho' now you may be forming imaginary alliances between _church_ and _state_, time has been when ye were nearly allied to church-mice.
>
> It is impossible to defend the system of disfranchising a fellow citizen because he is not so rich as his more favoured neighbour. Under any state of society property always has had, and will have full as much influence as it ought; and it is gross ignorance in politics to add so many artificial to the natural inequalities among men. Neither am I inclined to believe that public spirit and independence is exclusively confined to the rich; so far as my experience goes, the direct contrary is the fact: and I almost suspect it is as easy for a first rate ship's cable to pass thro' the eye of a needle, as for a man of large property to be a good patriot and a friend to the liberties of the people...

Early in August, it was Freneau evidently who discussed canals, denying the right of builders to take private land arbitrarily.[121] He ruminated again in "REFLECTIONS on several subjects,"[122] about the many rich blockheads, and the declining art of poetry, especially in America. He discussed the lack of impartiality in some new judges and juries, and the general lack of interest in being neutral in the European War, as the President's proclamation had declared we were.[123]

In mid-August---Genet having offended the administration, which asked for his recall---evidently Freneau defended him,[124] and then did so again.[125] In the same issue he spoofed the stars in a letter to "Mr. B-----" (Balloonist Blanchard):[126]

> As I understand you are making preparations for your 46th aerial flight, to the celestial regions... I send you inclosed a letter... it may be of use to you...
>
> At the beginning of your diurnal evolution, after you have passed the perigeum... through the different windings of the zodiac-circle, be cautious of approaching too near Scorpio.
>
> By all means avoid the Sun's disk, as its heat will be too vehement, and may scorch your silken tabernacle.
>
> Take great care of the Dragon's tail; fiery and poisonous effluvia issue from it. Tell Mars, our good and potent ally, to display his flag, and hurl his thunder bolts on the heads of the combined despots...
>
> Avoid Venus; she is a coaxing slut, and exceeding fond of silk petticoats. Greet the Planets, salute the Moon...
>
> If you see Enoch, Elias, Lazarus, Mahomet, Descartes, Galileo, John Clare, Tom Jacobs, Tom Godfrey, or Sir Isaac Newton...present my compliments...

During this month it became clear the city was infected with yellow fever. Soon a panic sent thousands fleeing; business came to a stand, and so remained through September and late October. 17,000 of the 55,000 left, and 4,000 died. With a rain in late October, the disease disappeared; and by early November, the legislators and most people came back. Nearly all the newspapers quit; but Freneau and the National Gazette, now without the support of Childs and Swaine, completed two years of publication.

Twice more the editor published his "Reflections,"[127] now

mostly political. He printed "Jersey-Coast Inlets,"[128] no doubt from his own observations. Apparently he wrote "Dialogue between a Citizen of Philadelphia, and a Jersey Farmer (ten miles from town)," rebuking people who refused to harbor refugees from the fever:[129]

> Farmer. Ho!---who are you, you yellow-fever-looking-fellow; and what business have you out of your city?
>
> Citizen. Sir, I do assure you, upon my word of honour, that there is not a sounder man in New-Jersey... Feel my pulse, and convince yourself.
>
> Farmer. Feel your pulse, Sir!---may I die by the grip of an anodyne necklace, if I would come within ten yards of you for ten pounds...
>
> Citizen. The sun draws low! A night's lodging in your barn... I feel weary...
>
> Farmer. Your weariness, or rather weakness, arises from the raging fever... Sleep in my barn!... my very horses would catch the yellow fever from you...
>
> Citizen. Could I have a bit of victuals for my money? The taverns are every where shut against us---a luncheon of cold beef...
>
> Farmer. For God's sake leave me; talking with you is like talking to a ghost---hoist your black flag, and away to potter's field!
>
> Citizen. I shall now depart... but not without first observing to you, that the common duties of humanity between man and man should have as much weight with a rational creature as the great duty of self-preservation itself... Cowards shrink from danger: the brave, when necessary, meet it with fortitude: and, trust me, you will find, in at least ninety instances out of a hundred, that cowards perish through the very effects of their fears, while the firm escape... Adieu.

The dramatic form was one that Freneau used frequently. An oddity in the above dialogue is the farmer's use of nautical terms, typical of Freneau. In "From the Archives of the city of Barrataria, 1693,"[130] a "Dr. Sangrado" flees the city to escape the fever. Both pieces satirize people for cowardice. Now the editor took time out to defend the theater, retorting to a preacher who had called playhouses sinks of sin:[131]

> Perhaps the gentleman does not know that a number of his own profession have given their countenance to the

> stage by their dramatic writings; or that the great Addison, whose character stands eminently conspicuous in America and his native country (and that among clergymen of perhaps equal goodness with himself) both as a man and christian, through all his writings speaks highly of a well regulated theatre... Can he with any degree of propriety amidst all his declaiming against its immoral tendency, suppose that there exists a single sentence in those two noble tragedies, Cato and Gustavus Vasa, the restorer of his country, that can have the least pernicious effect whatever on the minds of an audience?...

Though he printed the last issue on October 26, 1793, Freneau wrote his "valedictory" for October 19, reiterating his faith in the principles for which he had worked, sure the Republicans had won a great victory---[132]

> ...a great political reformation has within these three or four years past been gradually taking place. Aristocratical innovations are on the decline, and their authors and abettors grown out of all consequence with the people. In a great degree, this happy change may be imputed to the exertions of free and patriotic presses, operating upon the good sense of the great body of citizens... Go on, then, in this your useful line of duty, all honest and benevolent writers, printers, and editors! Though your labours may not always meet with their just and deserved reward, tho' yourselves may be calumniated, your views misrepresented, and your principles decried... yet by a prudent perseverance, despising their resentment... you will ultimately have the satisfaction to see tory machination and malice, aristocratical seclusion, court ambition, court mystery, court intrigue, and every other poisonous excrescence of imported royalty, withering into an eternal non-existence before that fatal scythe, which tyranny and tyrants never could withstand--
>
> A FREE PRESS.

Here, by indirection, Freneau explained the ordeal he had suffered as editor of the National Gazette. In the final issue he again criticized Hamilton, to him the symbol of American aristocracy.[133] He also reminded readers of their dues, his importation of "new and elegant printing types from Europe," and his intent to resume publication "in a short time." But the National Gazette was never resumed. Freneau took his new types to his farm in Monmouth, New Jersey, and there published an almanac, a new collection of his poems, and a rural newspaper for one year, the Jersey Chronicle, a weak echo of the National Gazette.

VI. The Almanac and the 1795 Poems

With his new types, Printer Freneau planned a country newspaper and in July, 1794, solicited subscriptions for a weekly to be called "The Monmouth Gazette, and East-Jersey Intelligencer." But the project fell through. Meanwhile, material was gathered for an almanac, which appeared as The Monmouth Almanac for 1795, published at Middletown-Point. It was unpaged, of forty-eight pages including the cover, and numbered "NUMBER I," in anticipation of a series. But this was the only Freneau almanac.

It contained the signs of the zodiac, the sun-moon eclipses, tables of the tides, monthly calendars, weight lists, roads, etc., weather predictions and remarks, with some fifteen items for entertainment and instruction: articles, anecdotes, and stories. Almost all were doubtless written by the compiler, with many short paragraphs about distances, midwest lands and lakes, etc.

No item is memorable; but "On Dogs" is eloquent. A few samples will reveal the tone of the whole. The following is from "Particulars relative to the BASTILLE of France"---[134]

> This famous building (demolished at the commencement of the late Revolution) was a state Prison, consisting of eight very strong towers, surrounded with a ditch about 120 feet wide, and a wall 60 feet high. It was first erected by Louis XIth, Anno 1460; a tyrant to whom an execution was a favorite amusement, who invented iron cages for the imprisonment of his subjects, and who never went abroad without an executioner attending him...
>
> The cells for the prisoners were very numerous, and were all contained in the towers, of which the walls were at the top twelve, and at the bottom forty feet thick. Each cell had a vent-hole made in the wall, but crossed by three grates of iron... Through these a passage was left to the light, scarcely two inches broad. In winter, these dungeons were perfect ice-houses; in summer they were suffocating stoves...

The longest article, "Of the PLANETARY System," illustrates Freneau's lifetime interest in astronomy--[135]

> 1. Space is supposed to be an infinite abyss, interspersed with innumerable worlds, each class revolving round some particular centre, and the whole round some common centre. The fixed stars, that is, those stars in the firmament which always appear to us to be at the same

> distance from each other, are no more than suns... each having a number of planets, or worlds, revolving round them, supposed to be habitations of various orders of intellectual beings...
>
> The chief error of the ancients, in respect to the Planetary system, was, that they imagined the great bodies of the universe much nearer to the earth than, in fact, they are; and consequently much less in proportion to it. They therefore concluded the earth to be of much more importance in the star system than in reality it is...

Freneau was a genuine dog lover, and his "On Dogs" is almost a poem, an eloquent tribute to this faithful animal that deserves preservation:[136]

> How many are preserved in their health and in their property by this faithful animal's services! The midnight robber is kept at a distance; the insidious thief is often detected; the healthful chace repairs many a worn-out constitution; the poor man finds in his dog a willing assistant, eager to lessen his toil, and content with the smallest restitution. Of all the beasts that graze the lawn or haunt the forest, a dog is the only animal that, leaving his fellows, attempts to cultivate the friendship of man; to man he looks in all his necessities with a speaking eye for assistance; exerts for him all the little service in his power with cheerfulness and pleasure; for him, bears famine and fatigue with patience and resignation; no coldness, neglect, punishment, or injuries can abate his fidelity; no distress induce him to forsake his master; studious to please and fearing to offend, he is still an humble stedfast dependant, and in him alone <u>fawning</u> is not flattery. All other creatures look upon man with an eye of <u>suspicion</u>, are with difficulty tamed to his service and discover no marks of friendship in their subjection. How unkind then are those who abuse and torture this faithful creature, who, with strength and activity sufficient to defend himself against most of the animal creation, has nevertheless left the forest to claim the society of man.--

"Philosophical Speculation" develops a pet Freneau theory, that people lived on the moon. He thought there must be an atmosphere there, and a central fire, as in the earth. What weird beings must live there!--[137]

> There can be little room to doubt, but that a central fire exists in the earth, which...gives animation to all perceptible nature thereon... That a similar fire exists in the central parts of the moon...I have no reason to

> doubt... What melancholy scenes of ruin and devastation do I there survey! What species of created being can possibly take delight in inhabiting those dismal abodes!...

Freneau's lifelong hatred for courts and lawyers, related perhaps to his father's loss of property by foreclosures, appears in "On Law"---[138]

> Such is the corruption of the age in which we live; that LAW and JUSTICE are absolutely different things.---The present system of law in America... confounding the reason of man, abridges his natural freedom... A lawsuit is like an ill managed dispute... the first object is soon out of sight... And this question is daily determined, not upon the evidence of the right, but upon the observance or neglect of some forms of the law... have I a right to eat the bread I have earned...? One grave law doctor answers me in the affirmative; another of them replies in the negative: the learned barrister reasons upon one side and upon the other, and concludes nothing. I... retain these three persons... My cause, which two farmers from the plough could have decided in half an hour, takes the court twenty years... I... have... a judgment in my favour. But hold--a keen scented lawyer... has found a flaw in the proceedings. I have used _or_ instead of _and_... and I have the whole of my successes quashed... Lawyers have erected another reason besides natural reason, and the result has been another justice...

And so on---with weights, coin values, state supreme court dates, Quaker meetings, town distances, and so forth, _The Monmouth Almanac_ filled its last pages. There never was a second Freneau almanac. The labor was too detailed and minute for a poet.

The 1795 Poems

His re-collected poems, his only personally printed edition, came out in April, 1795. He must have worked on them during much of the year before. The full title was "Poems Written between the Years 1768 & 1794." The book was composed mostly of items from the 1786 and the 1788 collections, along with some from the _Daily Advertiser_ and the _National Gazette_--about 290 poems in 456 pages. And unfortunately, some were personal barbs aimed at Fenno, Adams, and the Federalists, merely spleen verse, of no real value.

The author changed a few items and renamed others. "The House of Night" was reduced to twenty-one stanzas, and called "The Vision of the Night," with the death of Death omitted. "The British Prison Ship" was called "Cantos from a Prison-Ship" and arranged in eighteen irregular stanzas or "cantos." "The Indian Burying Ground," and "The Wild Honey Suckle," best of all, were fortunately unchanged. Yet, as a whole, the collection is rather disappointing; and the sales were slow. Doubtless many people remembered the author no longer as a romantic sailor-poet, but rather as a radical, a defender of Revolutionary France, and a scurrilous critic of Washington.

Meanwhile, evidently, he had been sending essays to the Aurora of Philadelphia, edited by a Republican friend, Ben Franklin Bache: two by "An Old Soldier" defending Genet;[139] one on Quakers and the theater,[140] by "Peter Pasquin;" an ironic plea that Bache join John Fenno,[141] by "Pluto;" one on the faults of John Jay (in England to make a treaty),[142] by "Philo-Republicanus;" and two by "Timothy Tinker,"[143] on the Democratic clubs. There was one ironically praising monarchists,[144] by "Benedict Arnold;" and one by "E." (a Freneau pseudonym), about Fenno's love for aristocrats.[145]

January's Aurora carried seven such essays, apparently by Freneau; February's, nine; and March's, three. In April and May, 1795, a series of three by "Yorick"[146] defended "Franklin" (probably Senator John Taylor), who had criticized the treaty with England. After May began, Freneau was too busy with the Jersey Chronicle to write much for Bache's Aurora.

VII. The Jersey Chronicle and "Tomo Cheeki"

The first issue of the weekly Jersey Chronicle appeared on Saturday, May 2, 1795. In his opening statement, the editor said:

> Never was there a more interesting period than the present, nor ever was there a time within the reach of history when mankind have been so generally united in attending to the cultivation of the mind, examining into the natural and political rights of nations, and emancipating themselves from those shackles of despotism which have so long impeded the happiness of the human species, and rendered the rights of the many subservient to the interests of the few...

This was typical of Freneau's international view--for the laborer, the farmer, the mechanic, the clerk, the lowly everywhere --and of his attempt to lead them into a life of greater freedom. But his audience now was rural, and uneducated; it was unlikely that he could sway his readers from the hard business of making a living.

In another article of the same issue, Freneau discussed the Jay Treaty (his sources at the time, mere rumors), his great interest being the liberty of the seas, an end to Britain's depredations on American commerce:

> Few of our vessels escape insult, and many suffer material injury: the Bermudians capture, libel, and condemn every American vessel they meet with coming from French ports in the West-Indies, and bound to the United States...

Another essay in the first copy, "Observations on the TREATY with Great Britain," also protesting shipping abuses, doubted British motives.

The second issue featured an article, "On Monarchy," criticizing kingly government and praising the republican form. An editorial argued that principles, not men, should determine government forms; and so it condemned birthday celebrations of public officials like Washington as being "royal" and aristocratic.

The third issue carried the poem, "On the Approaching Dissolution of Transatlantic Jurisdiction in America," a boast and a prediction---[147]

> From Britain's grasp forever freed,
> COLUMBIA glories in the deed:
> From her rich soil, each tyrant flown,
> She finds this fair estate her own.
>
> ...
>
> How small a part of that domain
> Is yet unbound from Europe's chain?
> PERU beneath a monarch sighs,
> And MEXICO in fetters lies!
>
> ...
>
> To abridge the sway of foreign lands,
> TIME, with his years, leads up new bands:
> To life, once more, some WARREN springs!

Once more, TO ARMS!--Fate's herald cries--
And other WASHINGTONS shall rise!

This is fair verse for mass consumption, but it lacks the delicate touch of the "Indian Burying Ground" and the "Honey Suckle." Yet if subscribers were thus led to expect many new poems, they were to be disappointed. The Jersey Chronicle was to be primarily a prose sheet. In the same issue was printed "Observations on Monarchy," condemning the worship of monarchs, even the great Elizabeth:[148]

> We will translate out of the works of an ancient traveller, his account of that excess of respectful ceremonial used at the table of queen Elizabeth, although not in her presence; and the kind of adoration and genuflection paid to her person, approaching to eastern homage. When we observed such worship offered to an old woman, with a bare neck, black teeth, skinny lips, little ugly black eyes, and false red hair, it makes one smile...

Freneau enjoyed discrediting monarchs, to show that monarchy was not glorious.

Another issue contained a new poem of four stanzas, "The Republican Genius of Europe," predicting the end of monarchy there:[149]

Emperors and kings! in vain you strive
  Your torments to conceal---
The age is come that shakes your thrones,
Tramples in dust despotic crowns,
  And bids the sceptre fail...

And an important first occurs here, an introduction to Freneau's best essays, "TOMO CHEEKI, the CREEK INDIAN in Philadelphia," a sequel to the short "Opay Mico" series in the Daily Advertiser---[150]

> Some years ago, about thirty Indian chiefs of the Creek nation, attended by several squaws, came by land to Philadelphia, to settle a treaty of amity...one of these chiefs was particularly noticed for the gravity of his deportment, his melancholy aspect, pithy sayings, and a certain exotic peculiarity of character, which distinguished him in no small degree from his companions.--- While they were amusing themselves in the streets with shooting arrows at half-pence...he employed himself in noting down observations on the buildings of the place, the character of the inhabitants, the policies of the white men, and such other particulars as occurred from a situation, to him, so new and strange:--- While his fellow

> deputies were carousing in taverns and dramshops, he would walk into the fields and woods, smoke his pipe---divert himself with fishing and such other rural employments as he found most inviting and agreeable to his savage fancy.
>
> So singular a character could not escape observation, nor do otherwise than excite some degree of curiosity. After his departure, enquiry was made of the landlord of the house where he had lodged... he was fond of cyder and small beer, slept but five hours out of the twenty four; rose constantly at the first dawn of the day, walked several miles before sun rising, eat sparingly, seemed generally absorbed in thought, now & then noted down his remarks in his own language, expressed great disgust at the manners of civilized society...
>
> The landlord added, that since the departure of Tomo Cheeki and his companions, a large bundle of papers had been discovered... The landlord having intimated that the papers were now his sole property, his price for them was demanded; and on being answered that he would quit all claim to them for the value of ten French crowns, the sum was willingly paid, as it seemed more than probable that the notes... could not but afford some amusement, if a translator could possibly be discovered...

This device of the "discovered manuscript" Freneau had used before, with the supposed writings of "Robert Slender," having perhaps borrowed it from Addison, who had begun an Indian essay series, but failed to develop it.[151]

The "translations" appeared in the Chronicle in fourteen parts till October 31, 1795. They are mostly a glorification of the primitive way of life, with criticisms of civilization. The first is typical, "Reflections on my first entering the great City of the White Men" ---[152]

> Here, then, am I arrived with my brethren of the woods after a long travelling of more than sixty days! Over how many rivers have we passed, thro' how many pathless woods have we strayed... directed in the night by the star of the North... and in the day-time by the splendid luminary of the universe...
>
> But what is all this I behold!---how changed is the country of my fathers! Instead of the green forests... here are wigwams innumerable, of immense height and size, and in comparison of which our council-house itself, and the grand wigwams of the chiefs of our nation are but the wretched habitations of the ant, the mole, the rep-

> tiles of the earth, the most contemptible insects and animals of the ground.
>
> These huge structures may be very pretty; but the first view of them disgusts me. Fond of the vales and declivities of life, fond of the fire on my own hearth, why have my countrymen sent me to sollicit trifles they might well do without, or necessities for which they have substitutes in abundance;---to make treaties that will end in our destruction, by bringing us into a more intimate connexion with the white men, who have ever proved proud, cruel, base, and treacherous; enemies to what they call the uncivilized life, promoters of wars and blood-shed, and the industrious distributors of those pernicious liquors, the effect of which has already devoted to death more of the original nations of this huge continent than have perished by the swords of a thousand invaders.
>
> What is this I walk upon?---not even the surface of the earth, as created by the great spirit, is permitted to the sole of my foot.---I dislike these pebbled ways, these little lazy channels of putrefying water, this cracking of whips; the anxious discontented countenances of all I meet; proving alas! too clearly that all are the slaves of care---care that clouds their best days...[153]
>
> A company of fighting men, led by a big-captain, advances to meet us: they conduct us to the town-house: I hear the sound of the drum: we are welcomed to their great village by the head men, and made to drink of their strong waters in token of welcome---now I am conducted to the house of a Publican, a man whose business it is to entertain travellers for their money.---I hate this inhospitality---it is not so with us. The man is cold, unconversable, and disobliging---I perceive already he is no friend to our nation---but the woman of the house is a young handsome squaw, and has already obliged me with a pipe of tobacco...

Thus we see Tomo already detecting some of the weaknesses and imperfections of the whites' city life. The second number is on the superficiality of the American Philosophical Society, the folly of its "research," and Freneau's deism:[154]

> I take the whole of this stupendous system to be a great machine, answering some prodigious purpose, of which the white men... have not the least idea.

The fourth essay, "A short talk on DRUNKENNESS," is an Opay Mico item from the Daily Advertiser[155]--not for abstention, but for a wise use of liquor. The next, "Containing certain Indian Notions and Reflections," dwells again on the whites' unnatural ways, and on human antiquity in America:[156]

> Men seem too much to have strayed from the grand simplicity of Nature in what they call their rural improvements... All is changed from what it was when the ancient red-men trod the gloomy paths of the wilderness... But CHANGE seems to be the system of Nature in this world. Come the time, it must, when the ancient chaos of woods will in its turn, take place of all this fantastic finery; when the wild genius of the forest will re-assume his empire...
>
> It sometimes makes me smile, when I hear the white men hold talks among themselves on the antiquity of this world they call AMERICA. Before the arrival of their ancestors on these shores (say they) all had been from the earliest creation a huge forest, inhabited only by red-men; by bears, foxes, and other wild animals.
>
> Why must I tell them that the most ancient Indian nations on this continent are but mere children in antiquity! When we travel through the vast silent wilderness, and far beyond the Father of Streams, the discerning eye beholds the places where mighty cities once stood... a numerous race of men seem to have flourished in this immense region, endued with the spirit and opinions of the white men at the present time; but the generation of red men came pouring down like a torrent from the cold woods of the north and the west, and bore down all opposition. The civilized nations were trampled under foot... We, in our turn, have seen ourselves become weak, like a tender infant---and after a time the Indian race will no longer be seen...

Archaeology seems to be in agreement with Freneau's theory, that before our present Indians, there were highly developed cultures thriving in what is now the United States. Tomo's sixth essay[157] is a tale of Moncachtape, an oldtime Yasou, and his journey up the Mississippi and Missouri, across the Rockies to the Pacific, then up the coast to Alaska and the Bering Sea. Here Freneau wanders from his original purpose; there is nothing about city evils and primitive benefits. But, in his next essay, he described a fine utopia of Indian natural living---[158]

> There sits the artist on his bench, pale as the grass beneath the thick spreading oak; actuated, like a machine, by the will of another; he moves not from place to place, but is restrained by an artificial necessity to his gloomy habitation.
>
> But in our country, and with us, a tree, on occasion,

will serve us for a house. Our largest wigwams are erected and finished in a day, and admit the light and air in abundance. In summer, we allow the winds to blow freely through the sides, made of cane and wattles: in the winter, the fire is placed in the middle, and all enjoy an equal share. Our woods supply us with plenty of fuel, and for nothing; while here it is brought... at the cost of much money...

But before the night is advanced too far, and the taper that yet burns brightly before me shall grow dim in the socket, I will put down some few particulars of the manner of what is called the savage life, by the white men ...

In the morning early we rise from the bed of skins to hail the first dawn of the sun. We seize our bows and arrows---we fly hastily through the dews of the forests ---we attack the deer, the stag, or the buffaloe, and return with abundance of food for the whole family. Wherever we run it is amidst the luxuriant vegetation of Nature, the delectable regale of flowers and blossoms, and beneath trees bending with plump and joyous fruits...

We are strangers to the cruel passion of jealousy, and consider that man as under the dominion of the foolish spirit who is distrustful of his wife. Our young women live constantly under the golden star of love; nor do we think the less of them if, before they are married, they indulge in that amiable passion.

In the forests, we acknowledge no distinction of property. The woods are as free as the waters; and the odious land-mark was never seen to arrest the foot of the hunter.

We are carried along upon the great wheel of things. We trouble ourselves not about the uncertainties, or the seeming irregulations of its notions. When the comet extends its long glittering tail over our thick forests, or when the moon puts on her black mantle of mourning, we apprehend no cause of alarm. It is the work of the great spirit of the universe...

However numerous may be our wives, or our children around us, we afflict not our souls with trouble to know what will become of them when we are no more... We leave them to the care of that good Being who is the protector of the destitute.

We hear not the voice of the tax-gatherer at our doors, to take away our bed of skins to support the luxuries of the proud, and governments that riot on the spoils of the poor. We despise all tributes...

Surrounded by forests that have no lines of boundary, we fear no storms--they blow far above us... We are in

> dread of no droughts, for nature has so overshadowed the soil that the sun-beams cannot scorch it... The most impetuous torrents are arrested by the woods and thickets, and cannot sweep away our harvests before them.
>
> Our manner of life renders us alert, cheerful, and courageous. We live in the midst of content, and when the time comes that we must depart...we depart without regret, because we are sure that our sleep, though in reality it may be long, can be, to us, but a moment... we suppose we shall soon revive, young, vigorous, and beautiful, to enjoy once more the chace of the forest and the pleasures of the wigwam...

Despite this fine idealization of Indian life, Freneau was only in theory a lover of primitive ways. He never tried to live in natural ways, but preferred to glorify "nature" and to condemn the city ways. He was not even a true farmer, only a resident on a farm. He was essentially a wanderer, with a preference for cities. In this delightful fancy, imagining the life of the Indian as perfect, very likely he was influenced by a recently published book, William Bartram's Travels Through North and South Carolina, Georgia, East and West Florida.[159]

Freneau followed Bartram in idealizing the Indians. Yet there had been many other influences in making a "noble savage" of the red man--and Freneau probably read most of them---to help create in him such an image.[160] It was a literary fashion of the time to glorify the savage as pure, above the petty faults of the whites.

In the tenth number, after discussing the Indian's inhuman treatment and superstitions generally, "Tomo" returned to the evils of civilization:[161]

> There is a little leaf, chopped fine and dryed, that is brought hither over the salt ocean in immense quantities from the very farthest ends of the earth--it is dry, tasteless, or at best insipid; but it is daily used in abundance at their tables here, from the highest big captain to the poorest artisan or labourer. Without this, life would be insupportable...
>
> But, of itself, this leaf is held in small estimation. Thousands of canoes must be again built and employed in passing to and from the sultry islands of the south, to bring back a sweet substance to make the taste of the

> leaf pleasant to the palate...
>
> Look at the labourer of the land. He rises long before the sun to attend to his cattle. He waters the soil with the sweat of his brow, and is ready to faint with grief when he considers that but a little of all this labour is for himself... When sickness or the accidents of life render him unfit for labour, there remain to him nothing but uneasiness... He is constantly encompassed with jails, laws, government, society... He is in want and penury amidst the amplest feast that Nature could set before him; and he is the perfect slave of error, passion and prejudice.
>
> Love itself has become degraded by the confusion arising from these invasions of the benign Law of Nature.--- How comes it that love, as things go here, is directed only by sordid interest... The multiplication of wants has debased the spirit of man... Cast your eye on that huge and glittering machine, drawn by six horses. I see three fellows, called footmen, stationed behind it, gorgeously attired indeed, but slaves in whatever light I behold them. Some great idol is within...[162]

In "Number XIII," Tomo addresses a squaw, Hopiniyahie, on the whites' vanity in publishing books, in finery, and in portraits ---[163]

> O Vanity! I find thee existing here in every shape, and under every disguise. Thou art found alike in the council house and in the cottage; among the great chiefs and the small artists; among the men of the law, and the students of the celestial science! Thou art found even in our own tribes... But I can forgive you, because Nature herself is a female, and fond of finery & gewgaws. Hence it is that she produced those gay flowers in yonder garden...

Here the writer veers from criticism of whites to criticism of Indians, and concludes that vanity is typical of all life, thus demolishing his case, in this one respect, against civilization.

In the fourteenth number,[164] Tomo predicts the whites' eventual self-destruction by war, and then, in a dream, foresees their destruction and replacement by a "ruling animal more perfect, more grateful, and more agreeable to the upright mind of the creating patron of the Universe." Candidates for the ruler of the earth were the elephant, the horse, the monkey, the dog, the lion, etc.; but all were rejected. So, in the fifteenth essay, new creatures were made---amiable, good, just, benevolent, busy in doing good works, having no slaves, and inclined to discuss God, the origin of the universe and earth, and the "perpetuity of felicity."

Thus ended the series. It began as a rebuke to the whites for their weak and evil ways, went on to idealize the Indian's way of life, and then to a condemnation of all humans--the only way out, their destruction and a new start with a new creature.

Despite its inconsistency and digressions, the "Tomo Cheeki" series is Freneau's best, and deserves preservation. Parts reveal a culmination of the "noble savage" ideal in America, unrealistic though it was.[165]

Meanwhile Editor Freneau was using the Chronicle as a text for instructing Jersey farmers in politics and government, with a bias for the republican form and a warning against monarchy and despotism. Some of the titles of essays are "Maxims and Observations,"[166] "On some of the Principles of American Republicanism,"[167] "On the Ingratitude of Republics,"[168] "A Political Creed,"[169] "Republican Liberties and Tendencies to Monarchy."[170]

Freneau had joined the general Republican (Democratic) criticism of the Jay Treaty with England, writing an essay on the British advantages in it,[171] and in the item "The treaty unmasked,"[172] etc. It appears that he sent at least one such essay to the Aurora, criticizing arguments of Hamilton and Noah Webster for the treaty.[173]

Other subjects touched on, May to December, include a satire on the treaty and the "kingly" ways of Washington, by one "Timothy Turnpenny,"[174] followed in the same issue by a defense of the President by "An Old Soldier"---evidently a bit of hedging, with some editorial remorse.

Another "Old Soldier" essay in the Aurora, to the President, defending France, was reprinted in the Chronicle, with the signature removed, a privilege reserved only to the author--almost a proof that Freneau wrote the "Soldier" essays.[175]

The Jersey Chronicle for 1796 began with an editorial praising Washington, who was soon to retire, and another defending Edmund Randolph, who had resigned the office of Attorney-General under pressure from the President, though apparently innocent of any wrongdoing.[176] But Freneau's interest in his country paper was waning. Farmers were never avid readers, there were too few subscribers (including too many non-payers), and they cared nothing for literature. Yet he did publish a poem now and then; one was "The REPUBLICAN GENIUS OF Europe."[177] Another was good, but unacknowledged; "Lines written some years ago, to the memory of CHARLES LEE," is worth reproducing. Lee was an eccentric but brilliant officer who failed to carry out a Washington order at the Battle of Monmouth, and later was court-martialed and dismissed. He spent much of his last years in vilifying his commander, yet in some ways was admirable:[178]

> Warrior, farewell! eccentrically brave,
> Above all kings, and yet of GOLD the slave;
> In words a very WIT--in deeds less wise,
> Forever restless, yet could never rise,
> At least no higher than to meet the ground;
> If strong the blow, the greater the rebound--
> Of all men jealous, yet afraid of none;
> In crowds forever--ever still ALONE:
> At once the pride and bubble of a throng,
> Pursuing rights, and yet forever wrong---
> By Nature form'd to pity the monarch's part---
> At best--A SAD REPUBLICAN at heart!
>
> But--to make known the aggregated sum--
> Above all monarchs, and above all scum;
> Unsettled virtues with great vices mix'd,
> Like the broad ether, where few stars are fix'd,
> Rest, restless chief! thy sword has taken rust;
> Peace to thy shade--and honour to thy dust!

The final Chronicle issues were largely filled with tales, like "A Jewish Tradition," and plans for "The Register of the Times," another rural paper, to be printed by the Diary of New York. There had appeared, in fifty-six rhymed tetrameters, "PARODY: On the attempt to Force the British Treaty on the People of the United States:"[179]

> AMERICANS! behold the fruits,
> The cost of all your vain pursuits...

And the editor took another slap at the public debt program:[180]

> Public debt's a public blessing---
> O the blessing
> Past expressing,

Never ending, still depending---
What a blessing
To be fleecing
All the nation, without ending!

He also published "The RIVAL SUITORS for AMERICA"---[181]

Like some fair girl in beauty's bloom,
To court her, see what suitors come!
An heiress, she, to large estate,
What rivals for her favours wait!

And he printed "Lines written several years ago," about a lover who had hanged himself, now telling his story: "Come--see the effects of Love."[182]

In the fall came an editorial in fulsome praise of Ossian, that fictional wild poet, once considered great by critics, but too, too romantic:[183]

> (The ancient BARD of Caledonia has been deservedly celebrated, as one of the greatest poets the world ever produced---he lived before the Christian Era, in an age when hunting was their support, war and love their glory, and poetry and song their amusement and delight. His images are lively and picturesque; his descriptions bold and sublime; nay, every scene he presents is a perfect transcript from Nature. A specimen of his stile we Present in the following ADDRESS TO THE SUN, which was never equalled, but by Milton, on the same subject; and if we deduct the advantage he derived from scripture allusions, we shall find him in point of sublimity far below Ossian.)
>
> O thou that rollest above, round as the shield of my fathers! Whence are thy beams O Sun! thy everlasting light? Thou comest forth, in thy awful beauty: the stars hide themselves in the sky; the moon, cold and pale, sinks in the western wave...

Jersey farmers could not appreciate this--farming is too practical for poetry. There are stray bits of unidentifiable verse in the Chronicle, and one Akenside poem, with a few anecdotes to entertain the benighted, also very likely wasted.

Nearing the end of the Jersey Chronicle's year of life, the editor, as usual, published his "Reflections" on life,[184] mostly political and critical of Britain and the treaty, of the tendency of the Federalist administration to favor all things British, and even of the general public love of money, a factor strongly influencing the lawyers and the ministers. He also aimed one more blow at Fenno:[185]

> Should Shylock publish you had stabb'd your brother,
> Lampoon'd your father or debauch'd your mother,
> Say, what revenge on Shylock could be had?---
> Too dull for laughter, for reply too mad---
> On one so poor you cannot take the law,
> On one so old your sword you scorn to draw;
> Uncurb'd,---then, let the harmless monster rage,
> Secure in madness, dullness, want, and age!

Freneau's expected next venture, the "Register," never appeared, and he spent the rest of the year looking for an opening in New York. He had some correspondence with the powerful politician, De Witt Clinton, and maintained a friendship with Thomas Greenleaf, Republican publisher of the _Journal_ and _Argus_ there.

Meantime, he apparently continued to send essays to Editor Bache in Philadelphia. The _Aurora_--which had printed "War! War!! War!!!" on the Jay Treaty, an ironic piece, by "A Friend to the Treaty,"[186] and a satire on Federalist Wilcocks,[187] both probably by Freneau--also published a series of Freneauesque essays in the latter half of the year and in January-February of 1797. These included one in mock horror at the French victories, by "a correspondent,"[188] a retort to "Phocion" in Fenno's paper, who had revived the Hamilton charges of 1792 against Freneau and Jefferson.[189] Also, in this group, there was an essay on war with France by "A Watchman,"[190] another on British schemes in contrast to French policy, by "An Old Soldier."[191]

The abandonment of the _Chronicle_ was sneered at by a writer in Fenno's _Gazette_. "G." replied in a defense of the Jersey paper and its editor in the New York _Argus_.[192] "G." was a Freneau pseudonym.

Sometime in the first months of 1797, Freneau arranged a partnership with one Alexander Menut, evidently a printer, who may have supplied funds for a press; and a new newspaper, largely literary, was to be started in March. In January and February, the _Aurora_ published four essays in the Freneau manner, with typical pseudonyms: "Semper Idem," "Simon Steady," and "Candour." Three satirized extravagant praise of Washington; and the fourth was a defense of Swift, the English satirist.[193]

VIII. The Time Piece, 1797

The new publication, a thrice-weekly mixture of news and literature, began with an elaborate title, "The Time Piece, and Literary Companion." A literary paper was a novelty for the American newspaper world. Evidently the original purpose was to stay out of politics and to mix the news with literary items, to inform and educate at the same time. But after September 15, when the Time Piece became another National Gazette, it was called simply The Time Piece.

The first copy came out on March 13. The editor, hard-pressed to fill his pages three times a week, reprinted his translation, Robin's Travels (1783), in serial form,[194] also the "Tomo Cheeki" series,[195] and many other items from the Jersey Chronicle.

In his opening announcement, Freneau again revealed himself, not as a practical journalist-publisher, but as an extravagantly romantic idealist:[196]

> The Editor deems it necessary to observe, that The Time Piece, & Literary Companion, will upon all occasions be open to Political, moral, or other interesting discussion, from any quarter whatever, provided such communications are written with candour, decency, and liberality, their object such as to promote the general good of our great confederate Commonwealth, or the common interest of man, and conceived in that disinterested spirit, which, while it carefully avoids as far as possible irritating the feelings of individuals, holds itself obligated in any circumstances whatever, to consider truth, the moral and political happiness of our species, public peace, social harmony, and good order...

Once more he addressed the public in verse, as in the National Gazette, in thirteen stanzas, gay and venturous:[197]

> Wherever our pages may chance to be read
> For the feast of good humour a table we spread--
> Let each bring his dish, and whoever may eat
> Shall have no just cause to complain of the treat...

Soon he published a new poem, "On the too Remote Extension of

American Commerce," in four eleven-line stanzas, a warning not to neglect business at home:[198]

Americans! why half neglect
The culture of your soil?
From foreign traffic why expect
Sure payment for your toil?---
At home, a safer harvest springs
From mutual intercourse of things,
Domestic duties to fulfill...

Next he orated in "TO THE AMERICANS," in thirteen four-line stanzas, on the fortunate situation of America, compared to that of other nations except France:[199]

The cause that rests on Virtue's ground
Shall potent through the world be found:
Mankind will bow to that decree
Which humbles vice and tyranny.

O'er this wide globe what darkness broods---
What misery, murders, wars, and feuds;
Must yon' fair lamps forever light
Man, to perform the deeds of night? ...

Freneau now published some inconsequential poems: on a western fiddler,[200] on a girl who wore lightning rods in her cap;[201] on Thetis;[202] another called "Dr. Perkins's Metallic Rods;"[203] and one obviously by Freneau, but unacknowledged, "Stanzas written, several years since, on the First American Ship (Empress of China, Capt. Greene) that explored the Rout to the East Indies and China, after the Revolution," in eight four-line stanzas:[204]

With clearance from Bellona won
She spreads her wings to meet the Sun,
Those ancient regions to explore
Where GEORGE forbade to sail before.

...

Thus, commerce to our world conveys
All that the varying taste can please:
For us, the Indian looms are free,
And JAVA strips her spicy tree.

Proceed, great pile! and o'er the brine
May every prosperous gale be thine,
Till freighted deep with eastern gems
You seek again your native streams.

It was a pet idea with Freneau that commerce was a way to

peace among nations, and this "hail and Godspeed" sort of verse was a favorite with him. Now he wrote an editorial, "Essay on Beauty," with classical references:[205]

> Those who adore or contemn Beauty ascribe too much or too little to the image of the Divine Maker. It is undoubtedly a gift, next to reason, the rarest which heaven has afforded to mortals. Plato calls it "A human splendor, lovely in its own nature, and which hath the force to ravish the spirit with the eyes."
>
> The judgment which we frame and collect to ourselves of the beauty of the spirit, because it is lodged in a handsome body, is not often amiss; and if it happen contrary to our expectation, we then say, Nature hath told a lye in such a person, the beauty of her soul being not answerable to that of her body. Beauty claims respect where ever there be eyes or reason, nor hath it any enemies but the blind and insensible.
>
> If the beautiful sometimes yield, it reflects not on the strength or power of that beauty, but on the weakness or depravity of their spirit...
>
> Nevertheless, it is worthy of observation, that Cato held beauty so high... he was heard ... to say, "It is not less a crime to offend beauty than to rob a temple." ...
>
> The beautiful ever gain their suit; and if justice ever opens her eyes to behold them, how poorly soever it is pleaded, their cause cannot go ill.

Many ladies of New York and nearby, delighted with the prospect of a city literary publication, and spurred by Freneau's invitation for contributions, thinking they could write poetry, offered their effusions, signed "Anna," "Cynthis," "Scriblera," and so on. They were answered by gentlemen like "Philander." At first, the Time Piece had a very numerous feminine audience; and the editor strove to please it.[206]

And so we find him presenting titles like "Equestrian Exercises at Mr. RICKETT'S Circus,"[207] comic verse on a fight between a lion and a turtle,[208] "Lines Written on a Passage from New-York to the island of Madeira, addressed to Calista on shore,"[209] "Ode to Friendship,"[210] and so on--unimportant verse, yet with some value in a sentimental way. And an editorial poem, pro France, revealed Freneau's serious interests:[211]

At every pore fair Gallia bled
Surrounded by her fiercest foes.
His well train'd bands proud Frederic led,
And thousands march'd where Danube flows;
While modern Britons condescend
To tyrants vile their aid to lend.

...

But ah! what valiant deeds have gain'd
By vile corruption's arts is lost;
The sons those rights have not maintain'd
Which were their gallant fathers' boast.
But Tyrants, sure, too late will find
Fair liberty above controul:
Her charms will soon engage mankind,
Though Britons, still, should condescend
To despots vile their aid to lend.

Freneau was never to stop hating Britain and loving France. This poem was printed with "On the Progress of the French Armies in Italy."[212] And presently his disgust with the orthodox clergy erupted in "On hearing a remarkably dull discourse, of near two hours in length, from a rambling lay-preacher in the back woods of North-Carolina"--[213]

Sound, without sense, and words devoid of force,
Through which no art could find a clue;
And poor, and shackling was the whole discourse,
That kept me, Julia, long from you!---

...

Ah Preacher!--with artillery like your own,
Hard will it be your <u>sleepers</u> to awake!
Trust me---although you fret, and scold, and frown,
You may beseige
But ne'er will take
OLD SATAN'S TOWN.---

Now came a long oratorical poem condemning slavery, "TO MATILDA," probably by Freneau, but never acknowledged. It is worth noting as representative of his lifelong disapproval of slavery.[214]

Ah Songstress, hadst thou <u>ever</u> felt
What 'twas to labor, pant, and melt
Beneath the torrid solar ray,
And wear, in anguish, life away;---
Oh hadst <u>thou</u> known the tyrant's lash,
Or seen the wide ensanguin'd gash,
Or heard the shrieks of agony---
Thou wouldst not plead for SLAVERY...

The poem was signed "The Slave." Another poem, obviously Freneau's, in twenty-four heroic couplets, unsigned and uncollected, is "Bermuda," with an editorial introduction:[215]

> Bermuda, wall'd with rocks, who does not know?--
> That happy island! where huge lemons grow,
> And Orange trees, which golden fruit do bear;
> The Hesperian gardens boast of none so fair,
> Where shining pearl, coral, and many a pound
> On the rich shore of Ambergris is found...

And an editorial in verse is "On the Proposed American Negociation with the French Republic." At this time our relations with France were very tense:[216]

> Thus to the verge of warfare brought,
> Our Congress takes a happy thought,
> Agrees half way the Gaul to meet,
> Prepar'd to fight him---or to treat...

Another retort to "Matilda," who had pled for the "gradual abolition of slavery" (June 7), appeared, evidently by Freneau:[217]

> Matilda may sing about slavery and slaves,
>   But what's the amount of her song?
> Why truly that mankind have always been knaves,
>   And it's right they shou'd always do wrong...

And in the next issue "The Slave" again replied--in 128 lines:[218]

> Oh why, if "justice" is their plan,
> Should WHITES retain their fellow man
> In fetters which themselves detest,
> And curse the hand that made them fast-- ...

On June 21, the editor changed the subject to kings and navies in "SKETCHES on DIFFERENT SUBJECTS"---the old kings fought in person; the modern ones do not do so:[219]

> What is a king of these days! a creature shut up in a palace, and kept almost as much in the dark as the grand Lama, the pope of the East-Indies... All this betrays a consciousness that a people are robbed of their rights, and assassination is dreaded... royal families have had their tasters for ages innumerable. They dare not swallow a mouthful, until a number of their attendants... have eaten several mouthfuls... Such is the picture of a king ---a being that... knows nothing of mankind.

Freneau had an unusual theory about the origin of navies.

They were created, he thought, in the search for an employment for nobility's children, in island governments:

> In insular governments... employment for the offspring of nobility was to be sought for on the ocean. The sea, at first view... is a field either of fishery or commerce ...Something more honorable, and consequently more idle, was to be contrived. Hence began navies, and artificial quarrels between governments to give those navies something to do...
>
> Previously to the attempts for an American navy, a race of well borns was to be found in our Republic, and we now see them popping up their heads like frogs in April from the fresh ponds, singing... War, war, war!...

Soon after the inauguration of President Adams, a crisis had risen with France; and leading Federalists, including Hamilton, clamored for war, and were raising an army and building a navy--hence Freneau's opposition to a "Federalist navy." Editorials on "war with France" followed, and presently the editor's mood changed to belligerency toward the administration.

July 4, George Warner orated in the city's New Dutch Church on "Means for the Preservation of Public Liberty," and Freneau wrote an "Ode" to be sung by the Uranian Musical Society, in five eight-line stanzas with choruses at the occasion. The song was published with the oration in a pamphlet:[220]

> Once more our annual debt to pay
> We meet on this auspicious day
> That shall through every coming age
> The feelings of mankind engage...

James Monroe's removal as ambassador to France gave Freneau another motive for re-entering the political ring; he defended Monroe's recent toasts, "Perpetual Union between the Republics of America & France," and said monarchy tended to harden "every gentle feeling of the human heart."[221] And he disapproved of recent British biography, probably with Boswell's Life of Samuel Johnson in mind, as "rendered insipid by a ridiculous and ostentatious display of the trifling particulars in a man's life."

Now Freneau returned to his old hatred for Fenno and the stuffy conservatism he symbolized. Retorting to remarks in the

Gazette of the United States about a banquet given to Monroe, he wrote---[222]

On a broom-stick from hell, with a pen in his hand,
Old FENNO came riding the air;
He look'd---and he saw that among the whole band
NOT A SINGLE APOSTATE WAS THERE...

Then, in a farcical mood, he printed a proposal, doubtless by himself, for paying off the national debt by raising pigs, by "MAT. MOONSHINE, jun."[223] Also, he rejoiced editorially in the English navy's mutiny:[224]

> Perhaps no class of men have ever been more imposed upon, or basely treated by their taskmasters, than the seamen of the British navy. They have existed under the most exotic of all tyranny...and have borne all this without repining...

His French bias now showed plainly; in August the Time Piece carried frequent quotations from Rousseau, Mirabeau, the Courier Francais, Gazette Nationale, Paris news, and French Traveller's Journal. Rousseau's Political Economy was featured. The Time Piece was now a spokesman for France and French ideas.

A long satire on President Adams ridiculed his love of pomp,[225] and was emphatic against tyranny, monarchy, and Britain. "Detached Observations"[226] discussed men's "revolutions of opinion" and said plays and players were being accepted, even popular, but they should be republican:

> 7th. The popular phrenzy in America, as far as regards sentimental pleasure, is in favour of theatres. Buildings of immense price are erected to gratify the public taste. But how is this pleasurable phrenzy to be turned to the interests of republicanism, and the good of mankind?
>
> 8th. THEY are much mistaken who suppose that buffoonery, double-entendre, and mere amusement are the real purposes of a theatre. Fancy and imagination among mankind are every thing. Aristocracy and Royalty by taking hold of these leading faculties in human nature, have rendered the theatre subservient to their own purposes. In a Republic like America, in whose exalted system the voice of all former Republics is "like the singing of frogs," the theatre (especially when countenanced by the public will, as expressed by legislative

> permission) should be a school of virtue and public good...

This idea of a republican stage Freneau had held for a long time, resentful as he was of drama's emphasis on royalty, a tendency that was to continue into the nineteenth century. In the same editorial he expanded the ideal of patriotism to world brotherhood, as a more proper goal for man to pursue. He did not cling to this idea, but soon fell back to patriotism and Democracy.

In the same issue appeared "On a Bee Drinking from a Glass of Wine,"[227] in six four-line stanzas, typical of Freneau's interest in small creatures. Now, discussing the origin of man, among other matters, he speculated on a descent from the apes, over sixty years before Darwin and the theory of Evolution:[228]

> Nature gave the rude outline of all vegetation, but left it to man to improve on her careless sketch. From the works of nature in animated vegetation let us proceed to man. He is the creature of improvement; he began in a mere Ouran Outang, emerged slowly from that state, & habits of barbarism; he liv'd in the woods for thousands of centuries; gazed at the sun; devoured the wild fruits of the earth, and slaughtered such animals as were within his power---and, when in want of these, drew the knife against his own species.---Hence, laws, civilization, and society, for the protection of the weak...

Many botanists and zoologists had long theorized as Darwin did in 1859 but very few writers dared to face an indignant orthodoxy with the idea. Freneau was careless--or bold?

Again the editor baited Yankees by publishing "The Old Connecticut Blue Laws (alias, Bloody Laws) were never suffered to be printed but the following sketch of them will give a tolerable idea of the spirit which pervades the whole."[229] Perhaps aimed at Noah Webster, editor of the rival Minerva; it included laws against new church members' voting or holding office; Quakers' voting; giving food or lodging to Quakers; the residence of priests; crossing a river without an authorized ferryman; mothers' kissing children on Sunday, etc.

Near mid-September, Freneau announced the dissolution of his partnership with Menut and a new one with Mathew Davis, followed by an oratorical "ADDRESS to the REPUBLICANS OF AMERICA"---[230]

> SAY--shall we pause, and here conclude our page,
> Or waft it onward to the coming age?---
> --Just as YOU say, whose efforts shook his throne,
> And pluckt the brightest gem from George's crown...

From then on, the *Time Piece* became another *National Gazette,* its main theme France, its main targets Adams and Britain. The editor at once criticized Webster's *Minerva* for objecting to foreigners in American journalism;[231] and he attacked Cobbett, the "Peter Porcupine" of Philadelphia, whose *Gazette* kept sneering at the Republicans, and had sneered at Freneau, who now classed him and Fenno together:[232]

> From Penn's famous city what hosts have departed,
> The streets and the houses are nearly deserted,
>   But still there remain
>   Two Vipers, that's plain,
> Who soon, it is thought, yellow flag will display;
>   Old Porcupine preaching,
>   And Fenno beseeching
> Some dung-cart to wheel him away.

Freneau was playing his old role of mudslinger. After another blast at them in the next issue, he wrote a poem in the same tone, "Melancholy reflections on passing by a burying ground in the neighbourhood of Philadelphia"---[233]

> What though made sacred by the parson's whine,
> Why sorrowing on these tombs should I recline,
> *Sheltering* some *Fenno* or some *Porcupine*?
>
> Wretches, who, breathing, poison'd freedom's air,
> Brethren in villainy---a goodly pair---
> But now are gone to print---the Lord knows where.

The editor was in high spirits, spurred by new prospects, or his new partner, and wrote a humorous essay, "*The sorrowful petition* of U, G, H, *to the American printers:*"[234]

> Your petitioners beg leave to represent, That they have always been found together in the words, 'th*ough*t, br*ough*t, s*ough*t,...' and they are alarmed to find that from the two first they are excluded entirely, by the greater part of the printers...

He could also find time for tenderness. Approving the French dissolution of convents and monasteries, setting thousands of nuns free, he offered a poem based on a true case, "a beautiful young woman who by the tyranny of a father was shut up in the monastery of Santa Clara, in the island of Madeira." It is a good poem in seven "Honey Suckle" stanzas, with overtones of Gray's "Elegy," yet unacknowledged; it might be called "The Lost Louisa"---[235]

Within the drear and silent gloom,
  The lost Louisa pines, unknown.
Fate shrouds her in a living tomb,
  And heaven, relentless, hears her groan;
    Yet, 'midst the murky shade of woe,
    The tears of fond regret shall flow.

Yon' lofty wall, that mocks my grief,
  Still echoes with my evening pray'r;
The gale that fans the trembling leaf
  Shall waft it through the realms of air,
    Till prostrate at the throne of heaven,
    Unpitied love shall be forgiven...

Now the frankly political editor defended the Irish immigrants, evidently as "Hibernicus,"[236] then poked fun at a printer's problems in the amusing "Ridiculous Distress of a Country Weekly News Printer,"[237] where a traveller helps "Type," the printer, fill his pages with all sorts of rumors.

In the same issue, "Petronella," evidently Freneau, authored eleven stanzas of untitled verse against the hated Cobbett, who is described as a venomous soul sought by Discord, urged to harry the Yankees, and found by Plutus---[238]

"Come out," cried the partial dispenser of wealth:
  While he gave him his gold-dropping hand,
"And get you away to COLUMBIA by stealth
With a period of wit and a column of filth
  And set up a press in the land.

"And still let it be thy continual aim
  To bring VIRTUE in general disuse;
Let thy cheek never feel the suffusion of shame
Though the WISE and the HONEST should caution or blame,
  But deluge the world with abuse."...

Once in a melancholy mood, like Shelley, Freneau dwelt on a debased humanity in "Reflections on the General Debased Condition of Mankind," four stanzas by "Z." (a Freneau pseudonym)---[239]

Is there on earth---or do we dream?
Is there on earth one power supreme
  That acts a nation's mind?
No---still oppos'd to human bliss,
All other views they blend in this,
  That robs and cheats mankind...

What are the views of Nature's laws---
What is the deep, unfathom'd cause
  That does her plagues prolong?
Nature, on earth, confus'd appears;
On little things she wastes her cares,
  The great she models wrong.
Z.

He reviewed Barlow's Columbiad enthusiastically and, incidentally, revealed part of his own poetic theory---[240]

> Perhaps no other event in the history of man, as a subject of epic poetry, has an equal claim on... genius, the emancipation of the western world. Poems of the epic strain... are founded on a comparatively narrow basis. The Rape of Helen; the Return of Ulysses to Ithaca... or the transferring an insignificant colony in a few barques from the Lesser Asia to the western coast of Italy, have been the subjects of those great master pieces of poetry, penned by Homer and Virgil, which stand at the head of all poetic excellence... how much the more should this sublime incident of our own times, the AMERICAN REVOLUTION, awaken genius... this STORY OF FAME, this real revolution, which, in its consequences, includes no less in the general condition of man, than a transfer from tyranny, slavery, and subjugation, to the benignity of rational government, equal liberty, and the advancement of that temporal felicity designed for man...

Now Freneau began The Book of Odes, a series of twelve poems, political and satiric, with "NO. I" ridiculing the Democrats ironically.[241] Some appeared in the 1809 and 1815 Poems. Their subjects included "To the Frigate Constitution," "To Duncan Doolittle," "On the Federal City," "To the Philadelphia Doctors," etc. None is memorable; the series is a tour de force in cleverness. A sample from "Ode XI," entitled "To the Philadelphia Doctors," will illustrate. Evidently his 1793 experience with yellow fever gave him no respect for physicians; he ridiculed the practice of bleeding:[242]

Ah, Philadelphians! still to knaves a prey,
  Take your old philosophic way;
When from the native spring you seiz'd your draught,
  Health bloom'd on every face, and all was gay---
Dejection was remote--and Nature laugh'd,
    A question now, of mighty weight is put,
    Whether, to bleed a man is best, or not,
  When scarce three drops (or not one drop) remains
  In the poor devil's veins!-- ...

An editorial, "Political Observations,"[243] asserted that a party in power must hold the national purse strings, that the wealthy always favor speculation, that indirect taxes are wrong, that the best governments make mistakes, that commerce unduly influences state policy, that tradesmen are degraded people, that commerce itself is a game of chance, and that it had become an engine of state, and that merchants always agree with the government. Such views help explain why Freneau could not succeed in business--he was deeply opposed to its aims and policies.

Freneau was a very productive writer in September, October, and November. Besides verse, editorials, and news, he did a series of seven essays ridiculing Yankees, those in Connecticut particularly, probably with the Hartford "wits" in mind--focussing on an eccentric "Hezekiah Salem." Salem was an ex-preacher, whaler, pumpkin-eating basket-weaver, living alone on Long Island and sending letters to the editor. His first was "On the Culture of Pumpkins"---[244]

> Pumpkins may be cultivated in almost any climate to advantage... Perhaps nature never did make a more generous present to mankind, in the way of vegetation, for food, both of man and hog. They will even make excellent beer... There is nothing in which a genuine New England man places so real an affection as in a pumpkin. It is the subject of his cares by day, and of his dreams by night...

Salem's biography relates how, as a preacher, he was caught bowling and dismissed from his church. He settled on Long Island, became a whaler, then a basket weaver, living as a hermit.[245] "Rules how to get through a crowd"[246] suggests smoking strong tobacco and chewing garlic, then whiffing the breath "out among the crowd," whereupon one is left in the center of a circle. Salem opposed duelling. Challenged by "Benjamin Bigbones," he agreed to meet him, if the local magistrate were willing, on the common before the public. Bigbones did not reply.[247] For music, he liked a "damp wind pressing around the corners of an old house."[248] A small man, he urged all small men not to be discouraged, but to remember the dwarf general, Tytoeus, the short Roman soldiers, and the advantages of shortness in travelling, going through doors, in bed, etc.[249]

It was evidently the editor who satirized John Adams, also touching on Noah Webster, in "First Chapter of the Third Book of Chronicles"---[250]

> But his heart became lifted up, and having amassed a great deal of wealth, he longed for the purple and fine linen of Egypt; and wrote and spoke in praise of their former tyranny... But the rich men did prevail, for they had silver and gold in abundance, and Jonathan was chosen chief magistrate... And after he had lulled them into security, he threw off the mask, and called the head-men together, and did talk to them of war, and fighting, and standing armies, in order that he might thereby oppress the people, and make himself a king...
>
> Now the rest of the acts of Jonathan--how he was worshipped, and the great feast that he made, behold, they are written in the book of records kept by NOAH the seer.

Doubtless one of the reasons why Freneau liked to ridicule Adams was the fact that he was a Yankee, along with those pesky "wits" and the stiff, unsmiling Noah Webster. Now in "Detached Observations and Reflections"[251] the editor remarked that "vice on the Atlantic coast" had greatly increased since the Revolution, implied that a close confederation made for a suppression of liberty, and said only dishonest rulers needed guards, that fear of government had no place in a republic. Also, probably he wrote "Incendiaries,"[252] by "Hotonthologus," which denied a charge that France had sent incendiaries to "depopulate our chief towns by the fever, and to desolate them by fire." And he began November by blasting the practice of duelling---[253]

> It is high time the system of duelling was at a close. There are so many evasions of duels at present among

> the choleric, that it is hardly worth while for a man of real determination to send a challenge. In the first place there is the justice of peace to beware of, who, upon timely notice, is ever on the watch to arrest duelmen. Some years ago two young fellows in North Carolina, to be in the fashion, challenged each other to fight by the road side in a pine forest, six miles distant from any house, for fear of interruption. No sooner was the first trigger ready to be pulled, than up started a justice of peace... It is high time the whole practice was done away. It is one of the horrid effects of monarchy and military governments, in order to keep up what they call a spirit of honour---yet they themselves are ashamed of it...

In Philadelphia, a parade was arranged for President Adams--and the "Old Soldier" spoke in the Aurora to warn militiamen not to join the display of pomp, and then congratulated them when few participated.[254] In New York, Freneau was angered at some of Fenno's remarks:[255]

> The objectionable ideas with him are, that every citizen, being equally a unit in society, has a right to a voice in the framing of laws, which are equally to affect himself and every other; and that the possession of property, being of itself an advantage, it is impolitic and unjust in a nation to add to it, at the expense of labour industry, and talents... To say that the placing of power in the hands of all must eventuate in laws exclusively in favour of the poor, as being the most numerous, is unjust and absurd... Who are they that would refuse to a poor man a voice in the framing of laws that are to affect him in common with his neighbours. The rich only--they are then interested jurors, and not competent to pronounce judgment...
>
> UNIVERSAL JUSTICE.

This essay shows an emotional disturbance, possibly related to the fact that Freneau was now fighting off creditors threatening to jail him for debt. The Time Piece, like other Freneau projects, was not profitable. Also he hated Webster for his attitude toward France, in respect to a royalist revolution there:[256]

> The intelligence from France, according to a certain sapient editor, is so extraordinary as to have astonished all descriptions of people. Even Noah Webster junior esquire joins in the general astonishment, and as usual attempts to excite the indignation of his countrymen against republican principles, by inveighing against the

> cruelties and excesses of the jacobins... Atheism and immorality, according to our ministerial creed, are terms synonimous with democracy. Will their parasite printers pretend to teach us that a reverence to God, and attachment to monarchy are in essence and substance the same? Is the jure divino title of monarchs once more to be rendered the standing theme of politics--theology and the pulpit... the detested instrument of royalty?...
>
> Democracy and Christianity are wholly incompatible! To believe in God, and to reverence religion must necessarily lead to a servile adulation of the tyrants of the human race!... This is the modern philosophy of our post deluvian Noah!...

Freneau was contemptuous of Webster, his love of pomp, as in his titles "junior" and "esquire," his love of money and his close association with business. Then came a condemnation of the "self-degradation" of statues, in an introduction to a French account of the demolition of the statue of Andrea Doria at Genoa---[257]

> It may be questioned whether in any case it be politic or prudent in a free people to erect statues to any human being, dead or living. It is a sort of self-degradation; It is setting up of images to worship...

Freneau may have been approaching a nervous, unstable state of mind, on any idea appearing to oppress the common man. He condemned Britain for glorifying war:[258]

> Human folly.---It is the pride of the British nation to talk of war, and their wooden walls. Let the question be asked, for whom is the benefit of all this war? Is it for the interest of the people? No! It was solely instituted for the purposes of the time-serving part of mankind, who, with a most ungenerous nature, by arming man against himself... have begotten wars... without cause or necessity...

It was probably Freneau who, as "Republican," criticized the President's replies to New Jersey addresses, especially his condemnation of "an enthusiasm for liberty too ardent and intemperate;" he said love of liberty could not be intemperate.[259] He objected to echoing Adams's speeches, as an "absurd affectation of the practice of the British parliament."[260] He attacked Yale's strictness (Timothy Dwight was president), also the students' retaliations on their preceptors, their tricks, etc.[261]

But the gay verve of the Time Piece was fading--its content was now strained. Freneau retorted to Fenno on deported British jacobins, against British injustice to conspirators--Muir, Margarot, Skirving, Palmer, et al were deported to Australia;[262] "Their open and avowed object was... to obtain... a radical change in the political representation"...

An interesting poem, because of the subject, is "On Deborah Gannett." This woman had served in the Revolution as a soldier, and asked for a pension:[263]

> With the same generous heat inspir'd
> As Joan of Arc, of old;
> With zeal against the Briton fir'd,
> A spirit warm and bold,
> She march'd to meet her country's foes.
> Disguis'd in man's attire---
> Where'er they fled, through field or town,
> With steady step she follow'd on;
> Resolv'd fair Freedom to maintain
> She met them on the embattled plain,
> And hurl'd the blasting fire...

Leary noted a change in the Time Piece about the first part of December[264] towards an unusual moderation. Years later Freneau wrote a friend that his enemies were then trying to give him "a seasoning in their lousy prison."[265] Imprisonment for debt was threatening him, and he was losing interest in editing. He wrote mild poems, like "On a Fly, fluttering round a Candle,"[266] and "Of Thomas Swaugum, an Oneida Indian, and a Missionary Parson,"[267] about an Indian who rejected the Christian heaven of "singing, and preaching, and prayer," and returned to his native ways.

But roused by the evils of imprisonment for debt, he wrote three essays, On Imprisonment for Debt;[268] the first emphasizing the need of sympathy and understanding, condemning the punishment, yet noting that willful debtors needed some correction. In the second he discussed ways of alleviating the prisoners' distresses, and suggested the "institution of benevolent societies." Probably he visited a prison or two:

> In passing through the gloomy apartments of a prison, many are continually descried who would willingly work, but cannot take in such tools as are adapted to their

> trade...others, the materials they have been accustomed to would not suit the capacity of the place...want of the most common necessaries of life is super-added to the miseries of confinement... See one in a corner, groaning in his distress, with a meagre, pallid countenance, and perhaps a wife and child... Another will tell you, I have seen better days, but my unrelenting creditor prevents me from earning by my industry... What signified bringing forward an American revolution, if its benefits were not to reach to all classes and conditions of men?...

In the final essay he proposed a plan: let master craftsmen teach their trade to the confined, their products to be sold in stores; the profits would repay the craftsmen. No word in the Time Piece mentions whether the plan was tried. Probably enough benevolent craftsmen were hard to find and any Freneau solution to any practical problem would probably be impracticable.

Near Christmas, a hilarious mood hit Freneau; and he satirized a painting supposedly of an eagle and Washington:[269]

> A curious composition of Architecture, Statuary, and Bass Relief, as it is called, has lately made its appearance before the public in the shape of a large print ---the original said to be drawn by a certain M. D. of this city... in the pediment of which is represented a bird which the maker calls an eagle... To this suspicious bird, on whose wings its author will probably take his flight to the heaven of immortal fame, I address the following ode...

Address to the New Invented Eagle.

Whether thou art an eagle, or a dove, or
A duck, a goose, an oldwife, or a plover,
Or whether one of Mother Carey's chickens,
Who ne'er appear but when the tempest thickens,
A dreadful thunder storm is at thy back,
And fate must reach thee from a sky so black.

...

O, Washington, and art thou here---
By heavens, I knew thee not;
Such a fine suit of blue and buff you've got:---
But why should each revolving year
Disfigure thus thy manly face?
Why drops thine eye a pensive tear,
That you, thus crucified, appear
In this unworthy place? ...

This was Freneau's last Time Piece laugh in his typical

humorous way. January 3, 1798, he sailed for Charleston, where his brother Peter would lend him the money needed to pay his bills. He returned in March, when he dropped officially out of the partnership with Matthew Davis.

But apparently he lingered around New York for several months, writing verse and political essays. One essay series, attacking President Adams and his policies, ran for ten numbers in the Time Piece, April to June, signed "Lysander," who was probably Freneau.[270] Also Bache's Aurora published an essay against an English alliance, by "Alfred."[271] The New York Argus printed several Freneau poems in June and July--on liberty, the republic, the prospect of war, democracy, political degeneracy--and the Time Piece printed others on the alien and Botany Bay. All are in the 1815 Poems.[272]

Federalists, trying to silence criticism, aiming at Republican editors, passed the Alien and Sedition Bills which Jefferson and Madison felt were not constitutional. But the summer of 1798 was a time of fears, of war with France, and of arrest for the outspoken who dared criticize the administration. So said a Freneau poem:[273]

> Last week we heard a king's man say
> Do tell me where is Botany Bay?
> There are, quoth he, a meddling few,
> That shall go there--and we know who...
>
> Be cautious how you talk so loud--
> Above your heads there hangs a cloud,
> That, bursting with explosion vast,
> May scatter vengeance in its blast,
> And send you all, on th'devil's dray,
> A longer road than--Botany Bay...

Freneau wrote patriotic essays now--"Crisis," warning of war, by "A Native American;"[274] one on British cruelty by "An American;"[275] one on the Alien Law, by "Montgomery;"[276] and two by "Democritus," ridiculing Adams.[277]

In mid-June, Davis withdrew from the Time Piece, and John Burk became editor--even more radical than Freneau; he was arrested under the Sedition Law, and closed the paper August 30, yet not before publishing his epic, The Columbiad,[278] worth reviving.

All that summer and fall, it appears that Freneau wrote for the Aurora essays for France, against Fenno, Adams, Britain, and the Alien-Sedition Laws.[279] Moreover, Doctor George Logan had gone to France privately, trying to help the cause of peace, had been attacked for it, and was defended by "Gag" and "Scourge," both probably Freneau.[280]

And the "Old Soldier" had his say in "Last Will and Testament of A DEMOCRAT, on a Sick bed in the last stages of an Aristocratic Consumption," satirizing Adams, Congress, Hamilton, and the authors of the Alien-Sedition Bills (Lloyd and Sewall of Massachusetts)---[281]

> In the name of ---- A----, to whom C------- have given all power amen, being of sound mind and memory, and considering the mortality of the body politic, and the uncertainty of my political existence, do publish this my last will and testament; I commit my political soul to ---- A----, believing in the Federal --------- which lately died by the hands of T. L. H. &c. for the political sins of the Republic, and its resurrection at the last day, the dead laws, and the life of the republic to come...

We were engaged in an undeclared war with France, mostly by privateers, but the public felt that a declaration of war was imminent. An army and navy were being readied; but Adams was a man of peace, and eventually made terms with France. Meanwhile, Republican writers were critical, encouraged by Vice President Jefferson. And Freneau's poems in the Argus were highly patriotic, tending to excite readers; for example, "The Republic and Liberty"---[282]

> Americans! rouse at the rumors of war,
> Which now are distracting the hearts of the nation.
> A flame blowing up, to extinguish your power
> And leave you, a prey, to another invasion;
> A second invasion, as bad as the old,
> When, northward or southward, wherever they stroll'd,
> With heart and with hand, a murdering band
> Of vagrants came over to ravage your land...

And in "On the Causes of Political Degeneracy," reviewing the tendency of the "base, designing, scheming few" to seize power and with priests to rule and make men "poor and mean," Freneau concluded:[283]

> Shall views like these assail our happy land,
> Where embryo monarchs thirst for wide command,
> Shall a whole nation's strength and fair renown
> Be sacrificed, to prop a tottering throne,
> That ages past, the world's great curse has stood,
> Has throve on plunder, and been fed on blood.--
> Americans! will you control such views?
> Speak--for you must--you have no hour to lose.

Such writings threw an onus of blame on Adams and the military leader, Hamilton, who favored Britain and feared France in the European war.

IX. Back to Philadelphia

As 1798 wore on, the Time Piece having expired, Freneau apparently drifted back to Philadelphia and, very likely working on the paper, contributed essays to the Aurora. Early in September, both Bache, its owner-editor, and his enemy, Fenno, died of yellow fever. Doubtless Freneau helped Mrs. Bache keep the paper going. Under "Reflections," he evidently protested the British treatment of American ships in the West Indies:[284]

> At a time when the indignation and resentment of the American people is incessantly excited against France, by every possible method, however just and necessary it may appear, great instruction may be drawn from a candid survey of the recent conduct of Great-Britain...
>
> It is a very deep injury to our merchants, and our country... and utterly inconsistent with good faith, that the sums of money, yet known to have been paid on account of all the appeals made to the London courts of admiralty under the British treaty, fall short of the interest of our spoliated property, and the charges of recovering it!... Just Heaven! we pray thee to save these distinguished States from a criminal acquiescence in such... wrongs from the king of Great Britain, if we should take upon ourselves in thy sight, all the solemn and awful responsibilities of a war, for the like causes, with an other nation!

Probably Freneau continued helping Mrs. Bache--as a sort of editor--till William Duane married the widow. Now he must have been delighted when young John Fenno, heir to the Gazette of the United States, announced his retirement. Five days later a sarcastic "epitaph" appeared in the Aurora, probably by Freneau:[285]

EXPIRED
On the 4th Day of March, 1799
At 5 o'clock in the Evening
Of a Malignant Distemper
After a miserable existence of 14 years,
3 months, and 9 days,
THE GAZETTE OF THE UNITED STATES;
Brought into being by the breath of flattery
and
Nursed in needy dependance,
Servility became its substitute for principle:
Without even the nerve of vice,
it was vicious;
Without any capacity to discriminate
between truth and error,
It became the organ of every one disposed
to promulgate falsehood...

The epitaph goes on to link the Gazette of the United States with Porcupine's Gazette, and pictures the funeral of Fenno's paper, with the pall supported by Federalist Senators and Representatives.

Now came an ironic letter from "A Monarchist,"[286] later to be seen as the first in a new "Robert Slender" series. But first "An old Ecclesiastic" took the President to task for proclaiming "a day of humiliation, fasting, and prayer," as taking an unwarranted liberty with religion---[287]

> I believe you are not authorized either by God or Man to interfere in matters of Religion... we have no national church... You have been pleased to direct the people what to pray for, and among other things "that he (i. e. God) would withhold us from unreasonable discontent, from disunion, faction, sedition, and insurrection."... who are the judges of the reasonableness of discontent, the rulers or the people?...

X. Robert Slender the Second

Shortly after "Monarchist" appeared, the "Robert Slender" essays began in the Aurora, and ran till February, 1801. "Slender I" --in a 1787 pamphlet and the Miscellaneous Works of 1788--was an eccentric bachelor weaver, lanky and thin, somewhat like Freneau's tall friend, Hugh Brackenridge. He complained of an author's limited opportunity in America, and criticized people and manners, but then disappeared.

"Slender II," in contrast, was a man of ordinary size, a much-married cobbler who talked at great length with a friend, "the Latinist," and assumed a familiarity with William Duane, the radical editor of the Aurora. His main purpose was to discredit the Adams administration, especially the Alien-Sedition Laws, to attack Britain, and to justify France; but he delved a good deal into Pennsylvania politics. His style varied from comic satire to patriotic writing; and his name appeared in some forty essays. Twenty-four were published together in December, 1799, Letters... of Robert Slender.

There is almost nothing worth preserving in these essays. Yet they represent a point of view largely typical of the Jeffersonians, and were largely responsible for the fall of Adams at a time of intense political passions. Slender probably helped Americans take a common-sense, humorous view of the international situation. But only rarely is a passage found worth noting. Too much space is taken up with Pennsylvania politics to be of interest now. Yet the name of the author has a certain fame.

1799 was an unpoetic year for Freneau. He expressed himself forcefully in prose under many pseudonyms, along with the "Slender" essays, signing names like "Simon Simple," "Veritas," "American Sailor," etc., mostly to political essays. Editor Duane had no taste for poetry, but he welcomed all pro-Democratic, anti-Federalist essays. One exception was Freneau's patriotic poem signed "Martial jun."---[288]

'Tis past--another Anniversive day
Has smiled upon our states, with UNION blest:
Pale envy, shrinking, hides her blood-stain'd crest,
And lurking slav'ry flies without delay:
And let her fly far from Columbia's coast,

...

Dear INDEPENDENCE ever be our boast,
Tenacious we will grasp thee to our heart;
Despotic power avaunt---we ne'er shall part---
Sooner our heart's best blood shall all be lost.
AURORA rise---proclaim to all we're free;
CREATED EQUAL, equal still we'll be;
And to posterity, without alloy,
Transmit a RIGHT which tyrants can't destroy.

A typical Freneau editorial, "Political Reflections,"[289] reviewed problems of the Revolutionary War and appealed for support of France:

> We had the general voice of mankind with us, for mankind saw us at a distance dispassionately... no misrepresentations of apprehended danger from the propagation of those principles which Plato and Solon---Cato and the Brutii---which William Tell and Barneveldt---which Sydney and Hampden---which Franklin and Samuel Adams taught... on the contrary we had with us the most powerful nation in Europe... What would be our state now, if France could be loosened in friendship...? ...

Freneau also wrote an elegy, "EPITAPH on MRS. H. RITTENHOUSE"---[290]

> If worth you honor, in this shrine repair
> Which holds the Relics of a Friend sincere!
> 'Twas her's with skill to regulate her mind,
> Where bright, superior understanding shin'd...
>
> ...
>
> 'Twas her's thus once to live--but now beneath
> Her ashes slumber in the arms of Death;
> While her blest Spirit from the rage of Time
> Rejoins our Patriot in a happier clime.
>
> L.

As "Timothy Deep,"[291] it was doubtless Freneau who recommended that the city replace water with beer, to prevent water-tax complaints, in a style very like that of "Robert Slender." As "A Refugee,"[292] he evidently satirized the carousing and stealing of the soldiers. And though he wrote two poetic tributes on the death of Washington,[293] he may also have done a satire on effusive elegies of the great man, by "Robt. Buckskin."[294] The poem by "Sylvius," titled "Stanzas to the Memory of Gen. Washington, who died Dec. 14, 1799," pays high tribute to the man he had once satirized:[295]

> Thou, Washington, by heaven design'd
> To act a part in human things
> That few have known among mankind,
> And far beyond the task of kings;
> We hail you now to heaven received,
> Your mighty task on earth achieved...

Thus Freneau repaid, in part, a debt of admiration to a man he had always admired, though he had ridiculed him as a monarchistic tool of Hamilton and the Federalists. And having seen, in a theater, a "presidential" adulation of Mrs. Adams, as "Cleopatra" he probably wrote this---[296]

> The occurrence has encouraged me to hope, that in future... Mrs. Adams may address the Legislature, receive their answer, send messages, confirm laws, nominate ambassadors, and in short do all the President's business as proxy...

He was evidently "Francis Foresight,"[297] who ridiculed the Ross Bill, to legalize the appointment of a President by Congress. Very likely, too, he was "Nathan Cornstalk," who ridiculed British impressment of American sailors.[298] As "An Old Rat-Catcher," it was probably he who advised Duane how to get rid of Federal rats--"put a bell on the old grey-headed rat."[299] On trips to Charleston, he wrote for the City Gazette; one of his poems there was "On a View of the Planet Jupiter and his Moons..."---[300]

> Proud planet! Are our eyes deceived?---
> Who has not seen, has not believed
> That in the aetherial, vaulted waste
> Spheres like our own, and worlds, are placed.
> Of bulk stupendous, mightier far
> Than is our earth, a meaner star;
> And Reason's eye, another race
> Of Nature's children there may trace...

The poet's fancy pictured Jupiter's genius objecting to man's prying eyes; if men got there, they might spoil the peace there, "would perplex, intrigue, ensnare," and make Jupiter into "the horrid image of his own."

The "Slender" essays appeared regularly at first, then erratically. Freneau and Duane made much of a sailor, "Jonathan Robbins," supposedly an impressed American who was executed by the British for mutiny. Freneau waxed very much excited:[301]

> Reader,
> If thou be a Christian and a Freeman,
> consider
> By what unexampled causes
> It has become necessary to construct
> This Monument
> Of national degradation
> and

Individual injustice;
which is erected
TO THE MEMORY of a Citizen of the United States,
JONATHAN ROBBINS, MARINER

. . .

Like him
You one day may be trussed up, to satiate British vengeance;
Your heinous crime,
Daring to prefer danger or death
To a base bondage--
Alas poor Robbins!
Alas poor Liberty!
Alas my country!

This epitaph was reprinted all over the country, and embarrassed Adams, who had delivered "Robbins" to the English for punishment. Actually, the man's name was Nash, an Irishman. But neither Freneau nor Duane ever confessed their mistake. Such is the integrity of poets and radicals!

Perhaps the most whimsical "Slender" essay now appeared, revealing the cobbler character who was supposedly the author of the <u>Letters</u>:[302]

> Having heard that there was a tavern at about the distance of a mile or so from my favourite country spot, where now and then a few neighbours meet to spit, smoke segars, drink apple whiskey, cider, or cider-royal, and read the news---a few evenings ago, I put on my best coat, combed out my wig, put my spectacles in my pocket, and a quarter dollar--This I thought was right; for although Mrs. Slender told me eleven-pence was enough, says I, I'll e'en take the quarter dollar, for a man always feels himself of more consequence when he has got good money in his pocket---so out I walks, with a good stout stick in my hand, which I always make a point to carry with me, lest the dogs should make rather freer with my legs than I could wish. But I had not gone more than half the way, when, by making a false step, I splash'd my stocking from the knee to the ancle--Odds my heart, said I, see what a hand I have made of my stocking; I'll be bail, added I, I'll hear of this in both sides of my head... Had I, said I, (talking to myself all the while) the disposal of but half the income of the United States, I could at least so order matters, that a man might walk to his next neighbour's without splashing his stockings... money might with more profit be laid out in repairing the roads, than in marine establishments... I looked up, and perceived to my surprise, that if I had gone but one step farther, I would

> have actually knocked my nose against the sign-post--- I declare, said I, here I am---this is a tavern indeed. I then felt in my pocket, if I had my quarter dollar, which to my joy I found---I then unbuttoned my coat, to shew my silk waistcoat, pulled my watch chain a good piece longer out of my pocket, fixed my hat a little better on my head--and then advanced boldly into the tavern...

From these remarks, it is clear that "Slender II" did not resemble "Slender I." But there is too little of this sort of thing; the cobbler is wrapped up in politics most of the time. The book of Letters ends with the election of McKean as governor over Ross. But the essays went on discussing orthodoxy's inconsistency, Christianity's cruelties, the worldly interests of preachers, Federalist lies, and the possible effects of Jefferson's election to the presidency on the country, perhaps civil war? And so on.

1800 was another presidential year--Adams vs. Jefferson--and many respectable folks were fanatically opposed to the great democrat, with the false idea that he was an atheist. Like Freneau, Franklin, Paine, and Washington, he was a deist. In November, 1800, "Slender" ironically defended his leader---[303]

> I have read...the most fearful threatenings that if Jefferson were chosen President, there would be a civil war... I trembled... when my friend entered... Let no such nonsense as this frighten you, said he, they don't believe their own assertions...the great body of the freemen of Pennsylvania are friends to Jefferson... yet... a majority of two in the senate say Pennsylvania shall have no vote--unless the representatives compromise...

In January, the Aurora printed a fourteen-stanza song, anticipating victory, "Jefferson and Liberty," probably by Freneau:[304]

> The gloomy night before us flies,
> The reign of terror now is o'er;
> Its Gags, Inquisitors and Spies,
> Its hordes of Harpies are no more!
>
> [Chorus] Rejoice, Columbia's Sons, rejoice!
> To tyrants never bend the knee,
> But join with heart and soul and voice,
> For Jefferson and Liberty.

Because of a tied electoral vote, Burr (running for Vice President) and Jefferson each having the same number of votes,

Congress was locked in conflict--anything to keep Jefferson from winning! The deadlock was broken February 17, Jefferson winning. But "Slender" made a last appearance, blaming Hamilton (who had been throwing his influence against Burr, as the worse of two evils)---[305]

> When the devil and A. H---lt-n are at the bottom of this ballotting; if this were not the case, could it be possible that men would so far forget the oaths they have taken to support the Constitution and act for the good of their country... ?...

This was the last of the "Slender" series. With Jefferson's triumph, there seemed to be no need of a Slender to attack Federalists.

Now the Aurora burst out in a wild celebration, and "Lines extempore on the spur of the Occasion" was probably written by Freneau:[306]

> The daring Feds have try'd, but all in vain,
> To hold the sword of power another reign;
> But better stars determined the event,
> And JEFFERSON'S elected President...

This was followed by a long poem, "Pasquin,"[307] ridiculing the losing Feds:

> What a plague do you mean? for to raise such a pother,
> 'Bout Pickering and Dayton and one and another;
> Are the great and the good, the noble and wise
> To be maul'd and mal-treated by men who tell lies;
> Cease your nonsense Duane, let our heroes alone;
> What a pox, can't a man quietly pick his own bone?
> Every paper produces a new consternation;
> No creature escapes; you reverence no station;
> Great Hamilton smarting with anger and grief,
> Would go to the D---l to find some relief...

Another followed,[308] "Extempore, on his excellency the governor of Pennsylvania receiving by express, the joyful news of Jefferson's election..." Then came "The People's Friend:"[309]

> No more to subtle arts a prey,
> Which, fearful of the eye of day,
> A nation's ruin plann'd:
> Now entering on th'auspicious morn,

In which a people's hopes are born,
What joy o'erspreads the land!

[Chorus] Rejoice, ye States, rejoice,
And spread the patriot flame;
Call'd by a Nation's voice,
To save his country's fame,
And dissipate increasing fears,
Our favorite JEFFERSON appears.

Jeffersonians really believed that by this election America had at last won its political freedom, true democracy. And when the celebrations had subsided, Freneau retired to his farm. His great political work was done. Still, apparently he wrote essays for the papers. But poems came fewer and farther between than before. His most productive decade was over. What would he do now?

Notes

1. Daily Advertiser (DA), Feb. 4, 1790. Leary, p. 446.
2. DA, March 10, 1790. In 1795 Poems as "Maryland."
3. DA, March 17. Leary, p. 447.
4. DA, March 29. In 1795 Poems as "Massachusetts."
5. DA, May 10. In 1795 Poems as "Terra Vulpina."
6. DA, June 11. "Virginia" in the 1795 Poems.
7. Evidently Freneau's. Leary, p. 384. DA, Feb. 20.
8. DA, March 4. In 1795 Poems as "A Batavian Picture."
9. DA, March 15. Probably by Freneau.
10. DA, April 28. In the 1795 Poems.
11. Probably Freneau's. Leary, p. 385. DA, June 15, 1790.
12. 1795 Poems, pp. 419-420, eleven stanzas.
13. DA, Aug. 23. In National Gazette as "The Debtor's Soliloquy," Dec. 8, 1791. In 1795 Poems, pp. 27-28. Not in Leary.
14. DA, Sept. 18, 1790.
15. DA, Oct. 23, 1790.
16. DA, April 15--also in Freneau's Monmouth Almanac for 1795. The Spectator ugly club is mentioned in numbers 17 and 32 (where the Spectator is admitted) also 48, 52, 78.
17. DA, June 12, 14. Probably by Freneau. Pattee, III, 24.
18. DA, July 5, 1790. Doubtless Freneau's.

19. DA, Aug. 21, 1790. Apparently by Freneau. Signed "Philo Scriblerus."

20. DA, Aug. 23. Probably Freneau's work.

21. DA, Nov. 1.

22. DA, Nov. 1, 1790. In MA, 1795.

23. DA, Oct. 21, 1790. Evidently by Freneau.

24. DA, Oct. 15. Signed "A. B.," a Freneau pseudonym.

25. DA, Nov. 16. Doubtless by Freneau. Dwight's epic is about Joshua and his bloody conquests.

26. DA, Dec. 14, 1790. Evidently an editorial.

27. DA, Dec. 27. Probably Freneau's.

28. DA, May 5, 1791. Probably Freneau's. Leary, p. 385.

29. "The American Soldier," DA, Jan. 24, 1791. In 1795 Poems.

30. DA, Jan. 26, 1791. Five stanzas. In 1795 Poems as "Neversink."

31. DA, Feb. 11, 1791. From the 1795 Poems. Five irregular stanzas, 44 lines.

32. DA, Feb. 26, 1791, titled "The USEFUL, only in Vogue at COURT." In 1795 Poems as "To Memmius; a profound Politician."

33. DA, March 4, 1791. Four stanzas. In 1795 Poems as "To Sylvius, On his preparing to leave the town."

34. DA, May 27, 1791. From 1795 Poems as "To a Republican, with Mr. Paine's Rights of Man." Fifty lines.

35. DA, May 31, 1791. Seven irregular stanzas. From 1795 Poems.

36. NYJ, July 16, 1791. In 1795 Poems as "Shadrach and Pomposo," pp. 408-409. Not in Leary. Pomposo is Adams; the wight is Fenno, editor of the Federalist Gazette of the United States (GUS), whom Freneau despised. "Pomposo" is a nickname given to Samuel Johnson by the English satiric poet, Charles Churchill.

37. He also wrote "Lines" to Paine, DA, May 27. See preceding page.

38. DA, June 21, 1791.

39. DA, June 28, 1791.

40. DA, July 26, 1791.

41. DA, July 15, 1791. Neither series was acknowledged by Freneau. But the essays sound just like him; as editor he had the power to print them; and the ideas are his, so that the probabilities are strongly in favor of the ascription.

42. FJ, Aug. 24, 1791. Probably by Freneau, signed "EPAMINON-

DAS." 34 lines.

43. FJ, Aug. 31, 1791. Very likely Freneau's.

44. FJ, September 7, 1791. Evidently Freneau imitating "Peter Pindar."

45. FJ, July 13, 1791. Doubtless Freneau's.

46. NG, Oct. 31, 1791. In 1795 Poems.

47. NG, Nov. 14, 1791. In 1795 Poems as "Epistle to a Desponding Sea-man."

48. NG, Nov. 17, 1791. 68 lines. In 1795 Poems.

49. NG, Dec. 19, 22, 29, 1791, Jan. 5, 1792. In a pamphlet with The Village Merchant, Philadelphia, 1794, and the 1795 Poems, with 26 stanzas.

50. Leary, p. 455. In 1795 Poems as "To Shylock Ap-Shenkin," pp. 404-405.

51. NG, March 29, 1792. Recognized by Leary (p. 202) as Freneau's, but absent from index and bibliography.

52. NG, April 5, 1792. Probably Freneau's; see Leary p. 388. 21 lines.

53. NG, May 14, 1792. Probably by Freneau--Leary, p. 388. 17 lines.

54. NG, May 17, 24, 31, June 7, 14, 28, 1792. See Leary, p. 455. From 1795 Poems. Separately published, Philadelphia, 1794. About 260 lines.

55. NG, July 4, 1792. In 1795 Poems as "A Warning to America."

56. NG, July 14, 1792. In 1795 Poems.

57. NG, July 18, 1792. In 1795 Poems.

58. NG, July 28, 1792. In 1795 Poems as "To Shylock Ap-Shenkin," pp. 397-398.

59. NG, Aug. 4, 1792. In 1795 Poems as "To My Book." 33 lines.

60. NG, Aug. 11, 1792. In 1795 Poems as "A Matrimonial Dialogue." 45 tetrameter lines.

61. NG, Aug. 29, 1792. 1795 Poems, as "To a Persecuted Philosopher." 27 lines.

62. NG, Sept. 19, 1792. In 1795 Poems as "On Pest-Eli-Hali, the Travelling Speculator." 6 stanzas.

63. NG, Sept. 26, 1792. In 1795 Poems as "To an Angry Zealot." 18 lines.

64. In the 1795 Poems. 30 lines, heroic couplets.

65. NG, Nov. 21, 1792. Doubtless Freneau's.

66. NG, Dec. 8, 1792. In 1795 Poems as "On the French Republicans." 3 eight-line stanzas, heroic couplets.

67. NG, Dec. 15, 1792. Four stanzas. In 1795 Poems.

68. NG, Dec. 19, 1792. From 1795 Poems, as "On the Demolition of the French Monarchy."

69. NG, Jan. 19, 1793. In 1795 Poems as "To Mr. Blanchard."

70. New-York Journal, May 11, 1793, NG, June 5, 1793. In 1795 Poems as "Ode." Later called "The Rights of Man."

71. NG, May 29, 1793. In 1795 Poems, pp. 439-445.

72. NG, July 6, 1793, "By his Successor." In 1795 Poems as "On the Death of a Republican Printer."

73. NG, July 17, 1793. From 1795 Poems. 7 stanzas.

74. NG, Aug. 17, 24, 1793. In 1795 Poems.

75. NG, Sept. 4, 1793. In 1795 Poems as "On Dr. Sangrado's Flight." 5 stanzas.

76. NG, Sept. 18, 1793. From the 1795 Poems.

77. NG, Sept. 25, 1793. From the 1795 Poems.

78. NG, Sept. 28, 1793. From the 1795 Poems.

79. NG, June 1, 1793. Tucker published a collection in Philadelphia, 1796: The Probationary Odes of Jonathan Pindar, Esq.

80. NG, Nov. 10, 1791. Not in Leary.

81. NG, Jan. 12, 1792. In Jersey Chronicle (JC), July 25, 1795, as part of the "Tomo Cheeki" series. Leary, p. 457.

82. NG, Jan. 23, 1792. Leary, p. 451.

83. NG, Feb. 6, 1792. Freneau followed Rousseau and Paine in such matters.

84. NG, Feb. 9, 1792. Editorial titled "Western Discoveries."

85. NG, March 8, 1792. Doubtless Freneau's, a "filler."

86. NG, March 8, 1792. Noted by Leary, p. 453.

87. An essay by Francis Hopkinson, "Speech of a post in the assembly-room," dated Aug., 1782, signed "SYLVESTER"--in his Miscellaneous Essays and Occasional Writings, Philadelphia, 1792, I, 252-273. See George E. Hastings, Life and Works of Francis Hopkinson, Chicago, 1926, p. 374.

88. NG, March 12, 1792. The poem had appeared in DA, May 31, 1791.

89. NG, March 26, 1792.

90. NG, April 2, 1792. A sort of editorial.

91. NG, April 26, 1792. Evidently another editorial.

92. NG, April 30, 1792. Editorial.

93. NG, May 3, 1792. Editorial.

94. NG, May 7, 1792. Editorial.

95. NG, May 10, 1792. Freneau's--very personal.

96. NG, May 7, 1792. Distinctly in Freneau's manner.

97. NG, May 21, 1792.

98. NG, July 4 and 7, 1792. Freneau evidently aimed at Fenno and his paper in New York, where he used titles for federal officials and their wives.

99. NG, Oct. 3, 1792. Untitled and unsigned. The essay tells of Klimius's visit to Mardak, where citizens must perjure themselves or suffer punishment. So he left the city, "where the only road to honours and emoluments lay through hypocrisy and perjury."

100. NG, Oct. 24, 1792.

101. NG, Oct. 27, 1792.

102. NG, Nov. 3, 1792.

103. NG, Dec. 5, 1792. Unsigned, like an editorial.

104. NG, Dec. 15, 1792. Probably Freneau's work. Articles by "Artist" continued on Dec. 26, 1792, and Feb. 13, 23, 1793.

105. NG, Dec. 19, 1792. A filler.

106. NG, Jan. 5, 1793. Recognized as Freneau's by Leary, pp. 222-223, but omitted from his bibliography.

107. NG, March 6, 1793. Though disguised as "From a Correspondent," it is evidently by Freneau. He had expressed similar opinions before--and he and other editors of the time habitually used such disguises.

108. NG, March 16, 1793

109. NG, March 20, 1793.

110. NG, March 27, 1793.

111. NG, March 27, April 13, 1793.

112. NG, April 20, 1793.

113. NG, April 24, 1793.

114. NG, May 8, 1793.

115. NG, May 22, 1793. Next day Washington complained to Jefferson of Freneau's way of editing, hinting that he should be dismissed. In his Anas, May 23, Jefferson noted this, but refused, saying the paper had saved the Constitution from monarchy.

116. NG, May 25, 1793.

117. NG, June 5, 1793. Probably by the editor. Sir William Herschel (1738-1822), born in Germany, was an English astronomer and discovered Uranus and two Saturn satellites, besides cataloguing many stars and nebulae.

118. NG, July 3, 1793.

119. NG, July 17, 1793. Untitled and unsigned, but evidently by the editor.

120. NG, July 31, 1793. Another by "L.", NG, Aug. 8, 1792, is credited to Freneau by Leary, pp. 211-212, but is not in Leary's bibliography.

121. NG, Aug. 3, 1793. Signed "Considerator." Probably by Freneau.

122. Ibid., unsigned. A "reflections" editorial.

123. NG, Aug. 7, 1793. Under "From a Correspondent," but probably Freneau's.

124. NG, Aug. 17, 1793. Editorial, signed "Alcanor."

125. NG, Aug. 21, 1793. Titled "ADVERTISEMENT EXTRAORDINARY."

126. Ibid., signed "An old ALMANAC MAKER."

127. NG, Sept. 11, 14, 1793. Editorials.

128. NG, Sept. 11, 1793.

129. NG, Sept. 28, 1793.

130. NG, Oct. 5, 1793. Untitled and unsigned, but evidently Freneau's. "Barrataria" is a touch from Don Quixote.

131. NG, Oct. 9, 1793. By "Consistency," doubtless Freneau's.

132. NG, Oct. 19, 1793. Untitled and unsigned, but certainly Freneau's.

133. On the idea that political-personal controversies are not eligible for a critical consideration of Freneau's prose, they have been omitted.

134. Monmouth Almanac (MA), sixth page.

135. MA, eighth to eighteenth pages.

136. MA, thirty-fourth page.

137. MA, forty-first and forty-second pages.

138. MA, forty-fifth and forty-sixth pages.

139. Aurora, Dec. 23, 27, 1793.

140. Ibid., Jan. 2, 1794.

141. Ibid., June 12, 1794.

142. Ibid., Nov. 18, 1794.

143. Ibid., Dec. 29, 1794; Jan. 27, 1795.

144. Ibid., Jan. 6, 1795.

145. Ibid., Jan. 10, 1795.

146. Ibid., April 30, May 6, 16, 1795.

147. Jersey Chronicle (JC), May 16, 1795. In the 1795 Poems.

148. JC, May 16, 1795.

149. JC, May 23, 1795. In the 1815 Poems as "On the Royal Coalition against Republican Liberty," enlarged to fourteen stanzas.

150. JC, May 23, 1795.

151. "Spectator No. 50." Tomo-chichi was a real character, a Georgia chief and a friend of General Oglethorpe, founder of the colony.

152. JC, May 30, 1795.

153. Freneau here pinpointed many characteristic "evils" of the city life of 1795, faults that turned certain people toward primitivism.

154. JC, June 6, 1795.

155. DA, Sept. 1, 1790. JC, June 20, 1795.

156. JC, July 4, 1795.

157. JC, July 11, 1795. The far west was then a land of mystery.

158. JC, July 18, 1795. Like Wordsworth and Coleridge, Freneau was probably influenced here by Bartram's Travels, which idealized Indian life.

159. This remains a popular book. Wordsworth and Coleridge read it avidly. Bartram lived with the Indians and idealized them. Of the Creeks he said: "They are just, honest, liberal, and hospitable to strangers; considerate, loving and affectionate to their wives and relations; fond of their children; industrious, frugal, temperate and persevering; charitable and forbearing." London, 1794 edition, p. 488. Of the Lower Creeks, he said: "They... seem to be free from want or desires... as blithe and free as the birds." Philadelphia, 1791 edition, p. 211.

160. See Montaigne's "Of Cannibals," Behn's novel, Oroonoko, Rousseau's works, De Lahontan's Dialogues Curieux, Voltaire's L'Ingenu, Colden's History of the Five Indian Nations, J. Warton's "The Dying Indian," Carver's Three Years Travels, etc.

161. JC, Aug. 8, 1795.

162. Probably Washington is meant. He rode in such a carriage, the only official to do so, apparently.

163. JC, Sept. 12, 1795.

164. JC, Oct. 17, 1795.

165. Freneau discarded this view in his old age for a "hard-boiled" attitude, like that of his friend Hugh Brackenridge.

166. JC, May 30, 1795.

167. JC, July 4, 1795.

168. JC, Aug. 29, 1795.

169. JC, Dec. 5, 1795.

170. JC, Dec. 26, 1795.

171. JC, Aug. 22, 1795.

172. JC, Sept. 12, 1795.

173. Aurora, Aug. 12, 1795.

174. JC, Oct. 10, 1795.

175. Aurora, Dec. 15, 1795; JC, Jan. 30, 1796.

176. JC, Jan. 16, Feb. 6, 1796.

177. JC, May 23, 1795, four stanzas. In 1815 Poems, revised and enlarged as "On the Royal Coalition against Republican Liberty."

178. JC, April 16, 1796. Not in Leary. In Time Piece (TP), March 20, 1797. Probably by Freneau.

179. JC, April 23, 1796. Credited to Freneau by Leary, pp. 267, 462.

180. JC, April 30, 1796.

181. JC, May 30, 1795, 11 stanzas. In 1815 Poems as "The Political Rival Suitors," greatly enlarged.

182. JC, June 6, 1795, four stanzas. In 1809 Poems as "Love's Suicide," 37 lines.

183. JC, Nov. 28, 1795.

184. JC, March 19, 1796.

185. JC, April 30, 1796. See Leary, p. 268; not in bibliography.

186. Aurora, March 23, 1796.

187. Ibid., April 28, 1796.

188. Ibid., July 29, 1796.

189. Ibid., Nov. 3, 1796.

190. Ibid., Dec. 4, 1796.

191. Ibid., Dec. 27, 1796.

192. Argus, May 14, 1796.

193. Aurora, Jan. 6, 1797, by "Semper Idem." The essays on Feb. 6 and 20, by "Simon Steady," and on March 9 by "Candour" were probably by Freneau.

194. Time Piece (TP), March 15-31, April 3-28, May 1-3, 1797. 21 parts.

195. TP, March 15-29, April 3-28, May 5-29, June 2, 16, 1797. Leary, pp. 462-64.

196. TP, March 13, 1797.

197. In 1815 Poems as "Prefatory Lines to a Periodical Publication."

198. TP, March 24, 1797. In 1815 Poems as "Commerce..."; in Contents as "On the morality of commerce."

199. TP, March 29, 1797. In 1815 Poems as "On the War, Projected with the Republic of France."

200. TP, April 3, 1797. In 1815 Poems as "On a Celebrated Performer on the Violin."

201. TP, April 7, 1797. In 1809 Poems as "To Myrtalis..."

202. TP, April 10, 1797. In 1809 Poems as "Nereus and Thetis."

203. TP, April 12, 1797. In 1815 Poems.

204. TP, April 17, 1797. Not in Leary.

205. TP, April 24, 1797. Possibly an imitation of Cicero--unsigned.

206. See Leary, pp. 274-275.

207. TP, May 1, 1797. In 1809 Poems as "Lines Written for Mr. Ricketts."

208. TP, April 26, 1797. Probably by Freneau. Not in Leary.

209. TP, May 10, 1797. In 1815 Poems as "Publius to Pollia." Love poem in heroic couplets.

210. TP, May 24, 1797. Unsigned.

211. TP, April 26, 1797. Probably by the editor. Not in Leary.

212. TP, April 26, 1797. In 1815 Poems as "On the Invasion of Rome, in 1796."

213. TP, May 17, 1797. 24 lines. In 1809 Poems as "The Amercan Demosthenes." In 1815 Poems as "On Hearing a Political Oration."

214. TP, June 2, 1797. Almost acknowledged by an editorial direction. A reply to a letter defending Washington's possession of slaves. 100 lines. Not in Leary.

215. TP, June 2, 1797. 48 lines. Resembles "The Beauties of Santa Cruz." Not in Leary.

216. TP, June 7, 1797. Thirteen four-line stanzas. In the 1815 Poems.

217. TP, June 9, 1797. The reply is too prompt for anyone but the editor--dated June 8. Three four-line stanzas.

218. TP, June 12, 1797. Not in Leary.

219. TP, June 21, 1797. The essay seems to be a turning point in TP's character, from a semi-literary to a political paper.

220. In a pamphlet bearing the title of the oration, New York, 1797. TP, July 10, 1797, song titled "ODE FOR THE FOURTH OF July, 1797." In 1815 Poems, pp. 110-112, as "Ode for July

the Fourth--1799." (The date is wrong.) Twelve four-line stanzas.

221. TP, July 21, 1797. Editorial.

222. TP, July 24, 1797. In 1815 Poems as "The Republican Festival."

223. TP, Aug. 2, 1797.

224. Ibid., editorial.

225. TP, Aug. 28, 1797.

226. TP, Sept. 6, 1797. Freneau's world position: "Man should be 'the citizen of the world,' not of Africa, Europe, England, France, or the United States."

227. In the 1809 Poems.

228. TP, Sept. 8, 1797. Under "Communication," but probably by the editor.

229. TP, Sept. 11, 1797.

230. TP, Sept. 13, 1797. Four eight-line stanzas. In 1809 Poems.

231. TP, Sept. 13, 1797.

232. Ibid., Three stanzas. Yellow fever had revisited Philadelphia, and dung carts were used to haul bodies away. Leary, pp. 287 and 465.

233. TP, Sept. 15, 1797. Five stanzas. In 1815 Poems as "On Passing by an Old Church-Yard," ten stanzas, impersonal.

234. TP, Sept. 15, 1797. Unsigned, but probably by the editor.

235. Ibid., Editorially introduced. Not in Leary.

236. TP, Sept. 20, 1797. An essay, probably Freneau's.

237. Ibid. "By a Traveller," a Freneau pseudonym. The poem, "The Country Printer," by Freneau, also features "Type."

238. Cobbett was an English journalist who played a Federalist role in America, but later, in England, became a reform leader. Not in Leary.

239. TP, Sept. 25, 1797. In 1809 Poems as "On False Systems of Government, and the Generally Debased Condition of Mankind," enlarged to eighteen stanzas.

240. TP, Oct. 9, 1797. Leary, pp. 295-296, 466.

241. TP, Oct. 16, 1797. The series ran till Nov. 15, 1797. Six items appeared in the 1809 and 1815 collections, three in each, under changed titles. Leary, pp. 466-467.

242. TP, Nov. 13, 1797. Four irregular stanzas. In 1815 Poems as "On the Free Use of the Lancet."

243. TP, Oct. 20, 1797.

244. TP, Oct. 23, 1797. Other dates: Oct. 25, 31, Nov. 1, 10,

13, 17, 1797.

245. TP, Oct. 25, 1797.

246. TP, Oct. 31, 1797.

247. TP, Nov. 10, 1797.

248. TP, Nov. 13, 1797.

249. TP, Nov. 17, 1797.

250. TP, Oct. 25, 1797. Adams's aristocratic book was Essays on Davila.

251. TP, Oct. 25, 1797.

252. TP, Oct. 31, 1797.

253. TP, Nov. 1, 1797. Probably by the editor, though under "Communication."

254. Aurora, Nov. 4, 13, 1797.

255. TP, Nov. 10, 1797. Editorial.

256. TP, Nov. 13, 1797. Editorial under "Communication."

257. TP, Nov. 15, 1797.

258. TP, Nov. 20, 1797. Editorial.

259. TP, Nov. 26, 1797.

260. TP, Nov. 29, 1797. Editorial.

261. Ibid.

262. TP, Dec. 4, 1797. Editorial.

263. Ibid. Four irregular stanzas, 54 lines. In 1815 Poems as "The Heroine of the Revolution. To the men in power."

264. Leary, p. 299.

265. Ibid.

266. TP, Dec. 8, 1797. In 1815 Poems as "To a Night-Fly."

267. TP, Dec. 11, 1797. In 1809 Poems as "The Indian Convert."

268. TP, Dec. 13, 18, 25, 1797. Signed "A. B.," a Freneau pseudonym. The style is Freneau's.

269. TP, Dec. 22, 1797. By "Jonathan," doubtless Freneau.

270. TP, April 17, 23, May 2, 23, 28, June 6, 8, 11, 15, 18, 1798.

271. Aurora, May 26, 1798. Freneau and Bache were politically in agreement.

272. Leary, pp. 468-469.

273. TP, July 16, 1798--"Botany Bay..." From 1815 Poems as "The Serious Menace." Ten irregular stanzas.

274. New York Journal, NYJ, May 26, 1798. From the Argus.

275. Aurora, May 30, 1798.

276. Ibid., June 8, 1798.

277. Ibid., June 8, 25, 1798.

278. TP, June 8, 13, 15, 18, July 9, 11, 30, Aug. 10, 1798.

279. Aurora, July 3, by "Richard Frugal," and one by "Fillip;" July 14, one by "Several of the Militia of Morris County;" July 21, one by "Timothy Tremulous;" Aug. 3, 4, 21, by "Sancho;" Aug. 13, one by "Obadiah;" Aug. 28, one by "Cato;" Aug. 29, one by "Mentor;" Nov. 9, one by "William Tell" and one by "Faley;" Dec. 5, one by "Columbus;" Dec. 26, 1798, and one by "Jarzy Blue" in the same issue.

280. Ibid., Dec. 26, 1798, Jan. 22, 1799.

281. TP, July 4, 1798.

282. Argus (A), June 16, 1798. From 1815 Poems as "On the Prospect of War, and American Wrongs." Twelve irregular stanzas.

283. A, July 7, 1798. From 1815 Poems as "Reflections on the Gradual Progress of Nations from Democratical States, to Despotic Empires." Nine irregular stanzas.

284. Aurora, Dec. 5, 1798. Full title: "Reflections on the Recent Conduct of the king of Great-Britain."

285. Ibid. March 9, 1799. Actually GUS was begun in April, 1789, in New York.

286. Ibid., March 25, 1799.

287. Ibid., March 27, 1799. Probably by Freneau.

288. Ibid., July 6, 1799. From Slender's Letters, Philadelphia, 1799, No. XII, as "Fourth of July--An Ode." Five eight-line stanzas. Not in Leary's bibliography, but see p. 312.

289. Ibid., Sept. 5, 1799. Probably by Freneau--who else, in a Duane paper?

290. Ibid., Oct. 31, 1799. A sonnet by "L.," a Freneau pseudonym. Not in Leary.

291. Ibid., Nov. 2, 1799.

292. Ibid., Nov. 14, 1799.

293. City Gazette (CG), Charleston, S.C., Jan. 10, 15, 1800. By "Myrtilla" and "Sylvius" respectively. In 1815 Poems, I, 154 and 156.

294. Aurora, Jan. 8, 1800.

295. From the 1815 Poems, I, 154-156. Eight stanzas.

296. Aurora, April 10, 1800.

297. Ibid., April 14, 1800.

298. Ibid., May 2, 1800.

299. Ibid., July 11, 1800.

300. CG, Dec. 20, 1800. From the 1809 Poems as "On a Nocturnal View of the Planet Jupiter..." 62 lines.

301. Aurora, Sept. 3, 1799. From "Letter XX" of the "Slender" Letters.

302. Ibid., Sept. 11, 1799. From "Letter XXII" of the "Slender" Letters.

303. Ibid., Nov. 18, 1800.

304. Ibid., Jan. 24, 1801.

305. Ibid., Feb. 19, 1801.

306. Ibid., Feb. 20, 1801. One stanza, twenty lines.

307. Ibid., Feb. 24, 28, March 8, 1801. Doubtless by Freneau. Pickering was Secretary of War and Secretary of State under Adams. Jonathan Dayton was Speaker of the House.

308. Ibid., March 3, 1801. Seven four-line stanzas. Doubtless by Freneau.

309. Ibid., March 6, 1801. Five stanzas and chorus. Probably Freneau's.

Chapter 6

Looking Back After Victory, 1801 to 1809

Vacationing on the Farm

The Democratic victory won, Freneau vegetated a while on the Monmouth farm, paid a few debts with the help of his brother Peter, and assumed a philosophical attitude towards life in general. He wrote an occasional essay, and contributed a few poems to the literary New York Weekly Museum. One has some excellent lines--"Stanzas on South Carolina:"[1]

> Here, rural love, to bless the swains,
> In the bright eye of beauty reigns,
> And brings a heaven upon the plains,
>   From some dear EMMA'S charms,
> Some CIRCE fair, that haunts the mead,
> Some HELEN, whom the Graces lead,
> Whose charms the charms of her exceed
>   That set all Greece in arms.
>
> And, distant from the sullen roar
> Of ocean, bursting on the shore,
> A region rises, valued more
>   Than half the kings possess:
> There, endless wastes tall woods display,
> Placed in a climate ever gay,
> From wars and commerce far away,
>   Sweet nature's wilderness...

So, South Carolina's charm for Freneau was more than the presence of his brother. This type of dreamy lyric was the poet's forte; he always did well in it. Now he was inclined to write reminiscent poems, like one recalling his own six weeks in the prison ships of New York in 1780, 'REFLECTIONS on walking over the ground in Long-Island, near New-York, where many Americans were interred from the Prison Ships:"[2]

> Along these banks, throughout this shore,
> And underneath the river, more
>   Regretted corpses rest,

More crowds by cruelty consign'd
To death, than shall be told mankind,
  To pain the feeling breast...

But the poetic urge had largely subsided, though Freneau evidently wrote now and then for Duane. "An Old Soldier" defended the replacement of Federalist office holders,[3] as a good Democrat. Freneau apparently sent a few essays to the Trenton True American, a strongly Democratic paper. One series attacking Federalists was signed "One of the Swinish Multitude,"[4] subtitle of "Slender II" in his Letters. In another, "A Jerseyman" defended the Jefferson administration.[5]

I. Back to Sea

Again in need, Captain Freneau sailed once more, mastering brother Peter's ships, evidently still writing for the Aurora and True American. A series by "Atticus"[6] argued for a democratic national bank, not a Federalist monopoly, apparently by Freneau. Poking fun at women's fashions (a favorite sport with him) was the theme of "D. K.," answered by "F----- P------"[7] (P. F. reversed?). And "Barnaby Bodkin," a tailor, talked politics in the "Slender" style:[8]

> I was just pressing off a coat for my neighbor Candidus, as your paper of the 20th arrived... He is what may be called a very clever sort of a man, but he cannot get over some of his old prejudices against Democrats... He often told me he had read in the good federal papers, that the Democrats wanted to destroy all religion, order, and government; and to bring about anarchy, and I don't know what all... said I, I've just been looking over a document, as it's called, from a member of congress, in which it is stated that the savings... is upwards of three millions of dollars...

On one of his voyages, Freneau was impressed by Madeira, and wrote on the storm and flood there in October, 1803, "Stanzas Written at the Island of Madeira...", in the favorite "Honey Suckle" stanza form--[9]

From hills beyond the clouds that soar,
  The vaults of heaven, the torrents run,
And rushing with resistless power,
  Assail'd the island of the sun:

Fond nature saw the blasted vine,
And seem'd to sicken and repine.

...

The bursting rains in seas descend,
Machico heard the distant roar,
And lightnings, while the heavens they rend,
Show'd ruin marching to the shore:
Egyptian darkness brought her gloom
And fear foreboded nature's doom...

Another poem about Teneriffe was written a few months later, "Stanzas written at Oratava, in view of the Peak of Teneriffe, 1804"--[10]

No mean, no human artist laid
The base of this prodigious pile,
The towering peak--but nature said,
Let this adorn Tenaria's isle;
And be my work for ages found
The polar star to islands round.

...

For torrents from the mountain came:
What molten floods were seen to glow!
Expanded sheets of vivid flame,
To inundate the world below!
These, older than the historian's page,
Once bellow'd forth vext nature's rage...

Such "dream impressions" of faraway places, especially in mild climates, were a hobby with Freneau. The dream of living there, far from the winters of Jersey, he had cherished since early youth. This year, 1804, "on vacation," he entered the Philadelphia intra-Democratic quarrel, Duane against Tench Coxe, who boosted a William Penrose for Congress against the incumbent, Leib. In twenty "Slenderized" essays by the "Bunker" family, he aimed most of his ridicule at Coxe, a political economist, appointed by Jefferson to be purveyor of supplies. Freneau had a contempt for Coxe like that which he had held for Fenno. Here "Jonathan Bunker" sounds exactly like "Slender II:"[11]

> Our country, Mr. Duane, was once governed by federalists, who would have done very well, had they placed such men as Mr. Coxe in their front rank... Mr. Jefferson is, in my mind, responsible for keeping Mr. Coxe in the back ground... Already, sir, we have discovered three great objections to Mr. Jefferson... by

> procuring Louisiana. The Roman empire fell because it was too unwieldy... Mr. Jefferson is a friend to emigrants... the Romans had their Goths and Vandals, and we have the Irish and Germans...

And Jonathan reveals himself as a much-married man--[12]

> Last Sunday, after my dear Polly Bunker had washed up the dinner things, says she--"Jon'than, won't you take us to see uncle Simon, its mortal long since aunt Sally and I talked over matters and things." Being very fond of smoking my pipe after dinner, I made many objections. "Polly," says I, "we'll have a storm, its very hot now, so we'd better stay at home and go next Sunday, early." But, you know very well, Mr. Duane, women will have their way, right or wrong...

On the eve of the election--which Leib won--"Tomo Cheeki" (a sure sign of Freneau) called Coxe a liar and no gentleman.[13] But the squabble was intra-party and of no great consequence. After it was over, a series defending Burr in his fatal duel with Hamilton sounds very much like Freneau, and is signed "Sylvius," one of his pseudonyms:[14]

> Gouverneur Morris...extenuates the political hostility of the deceased to the principles of our government; and in a most artful manner draws the hearers into a contemplation of his eloquence, his social virtues, his generosity, and his humanity...charges them...that they will take care to confide their political rights to none except those who profess similar sentiments!!!... New York may thereby become a second MECCA, the resort of hypocrites paying homage at the shrine of imposture--and there knaves and fools may play their respective parts... Such was once the case at Rome. Julius Caesar was their God; then it was that a few who knew him only as a man and as an usurper, conspired his death...

After a half-year interlude, Freneau apparently resumed his Aurora essays, under new pseudonyms, mostly on state politics, now criticizing Governor McKean, with whom Duane had disagreed. No published poems are found for 1805---Captain Freneau was sailing again, and continued till late in 1807, when Jefferson's Embargo Act, confining our ships to their harbors, forced him back to the farm at Monmouth.

Now having heard that a new edition of his poems was being started in Philadelphia, to help Mrs. Lydia Bailey (operating the

Bailey Press), he came to the city to supervise it in the summer of 1808. At once the Aurora blossomed with Freneauesque essays signed by typical pseudonyms--"Juba,"[15] "Yorick,"[16] "Nauticus,"[17] and "Old Soldier."[18]

"Juba" defended the Jefferson administration and attacked Ross, Federalist candidate for governor--it was another presidential year--as did "Yorick." "Nauticus" condemned violations of the Embargo Act---[17]

> This villainous conduct calls for the decisive interference of the general government, and an immediate revival of the embargo laws. A most strict scrutiny should take place whenever a venal attempt is made to load or clear out... The punishment of an evasion by carrying a vessel to a foreign port should, with propriety, be extended even to death, as an act of piracy...

"Old Soldier" criticized King George and the Federalists, and advised war on England; in fact, this idea was increasingly popular:[19]

> It will not be denied... that the character of that nation [Britain] is totally changed... they have made open war upon all the nations who have sought to preserve the blessings of civilization, or who have shown spirit to resist them... if you don't see the immediate necessity of declaring war against that country, you are ignorant of their character, and blind to the interest and safety of your own.

Early in 1809, Aurora essays evidently by Freneau were signed "Warren,"[20] "The American,"[21] "Timon,"[22] "A Federalist,"[23] etc. Now the defense of the Embargo became a dominant topic. Madison, Freneau's old friend, had become President, and he was beset with demands to repeal the act. In March, "Old Soldier" said that war with Britain was inevitable, and "the longer it is delayed the heavier it will come."[24] A series of essays by "Chares" also attacked Britain at some length, and declared the Embargo a success.[25]

Freneau wrote an elaborate poetic tribute to Jefferson as he retired, "Lines Addressed to Mr. Jefferson, on his Approaching Retirement from the Presidency of the United States," ninety-four lines of heroic couplets:[26]

From your sage counsels what effects arise!
The vengeful Briton from our waters flies;
His thundering ships no more our coasts assail,
But seize the advantage of the western gale...

Long in the councils of your native land,
We saw you cool, unchanged, intrepid, stand:
When the firm CONGRESS, still too firm to yield,
Stay'd masters of the long contested field,
Your wisdom aided, what their counsels framed--
By you the murdering savages were tamed--
That INDEPENDENCE we had sworn to gain,
By you asserted (nor DECLARED in vain)
We seized, triumphant, from a tyrant's throne,
And Britain totter'd when the work was done.

Freneau could not resist showing Jefferson's influence for unity, and discrediting Hamilton and his 1792 charges:

You, when an angry faction vex'd the age,
Rose to your place at once, and check'd their rage.
The envenom'd shafts of malice you defied,
And turn'd all projects of revolt aside:--
We saw you libell'd by the worst of men,
While hell's red lamp hung quivering o'er his pen...

On Tom Paine's death (June 8), he wrote a simple tribute, "Stanzas on the Decease of Thomas Paine, Who Died at New York, on the 8th of June, 1809"--[27]

Princes and kings decay and die
And, instant, rise again:
But this is not the case, trust me,
With men like THOMAS PAINE.

In vain the democratic host
His equal would attain:
For years to come they will not boast
A second Thomas Paine...

Paine had done more than any other writer to galvanize Americans into a successful fighting spirit in the Revolution, and had defended democracy and the French Revolution in his Rights of Man. But he had also written The Age of Reason, which denied Christianity though it declared for one God, as he was a deist. He was labelled an atheist--quite untrue--ostracized, and abused. He died in poverty and obscurity. Yet he was a godly man. Freneau admired and followed him.

II. The 1809 Poems

From a Freneau letter to Madison, it is probable that the 1809 Poems were on sale in August, 1809. From a printer's view, the edition is the best of the author's career, well printed in two volumes, a frontispiece in each. From a commercial view, it was a success; over 1600 sets were placed.

But from a literary view, it is like another 1795 edition--primarily a collection of poems written in the Revolution and to 1793--to which are added some translations and other items. The volumes are divided into Book I, translations "and other pieces" to page 136, including "The Rising Glory of America" and "The Pictures of Columbus;" and Book II, "original pieces" and some poems on the Revolution, to page 280, the end of the first volume. This volume contains "The Indian Burying Ground," "The Vision of the Night" (a fragment of "The House of Night"), "The Wild Honey Suckle," "General Gage's Soliloquy," "The Midnight Consultations: or, a trip to Boston," "The Beauties of Santa Cruz," "America Independent," "The Prophecy of King Tammany," and "Sketches of American History."

Book III, which begins the second volume, to page 176, contains "A Dialogue between George and Fox," "The British Prison Ship," "On the Fall of Gen. Earl Cornwallis," "To the Memory of the Brave Americans" ("Eutaw Springs"), "Rivington's Last Will and Testament," "Hugh Gaine's Life," and "The Hurricane." Book IV, of "miscellaneous pieces," rounds out the collection, pages 177-302 of the second volume. It includes "Written at Port Royal," "Literary Importation," "Balloons," "Fancy's Ramble," "Pennsylvania," "The Distrest Theatre," "On the Death of Dr. Benjamin Franklin," "To Sylvius: on the Folly of Writing Poetry," "On the Approaching Dissolution of Transatlantic Jurisdiction in America," "On Mr. Paine's Rights of Man," and "Stanzas Published at the Procession to the Tomb of the Patriots."

Altogether there are one hundred seventy-eight poems. One wise move was to omit most of the bitter political verse of 1782-3 and 1792-3. The preface says the contents were written "between the years 1768 and 1793"--though the first part of the title is "Poems Written and Published during the American Revolutionary War." The preface adds that the 1786 and 1795 editions were sources, but omits mention of the 1788 edition, from which some poems were taken. For its time it was a creditable performance. And because the time was ripe for a patriotic collection--hatred for Britain was rising--the public welcomed it. Yet it was chiefly an echo out of the past. The Federalist press was silent about it,[28] probably because it was partisan and relatively coarse.

One of the new poems--though none was memorable--serves to emphasize Freneau's increasing tendency to reflect on the past and to philosophize. It is "The origin of Wars," in nine stanzas--[29]

> In early time, when man was blest
> With constant spring and summer joined,
> Nature his simple banquet drest;
> Long life was his, with health combined.
>
> In innocence (their sole defence)
> They spent their days, and passed their nights:
> In rural haunts they pitched their tents--
> None stole their sweets, or seized their rights...
>
> JOVE saw the vast abounding race,
> And feared a change in Nature's plan,
> That the wide world would find a place
> In one age more, for nought but MAN.
>
> Then thus of gods and men the sire
> In Vulcan's ear his mind expressed---
> "Wars must be had---go, fetch that fire
> Which kindles rancour in the breast..."

And, surprisingly, he chose to perpetuate a revealing poem--"To Lydia"--about a beautiful girl with whom he once fell in love--[30]

> On you all eyes delight to gaze,
> All tongues are lavish in your praise;
> With you no beauty can compare,
> Nor GEORGIA boast one flower so fair.
>
> ...
>
> To all your questions--every sigh!
> I still will make a kind reply
> Give all you ask, each whim allow,
> And change my style to thee and thou.

If verse can life to beauty give,
For ages I can make you live,
Beyond the stars, triumphant, rise
While Cynthia's tomb neglected lies:

...

Then, Lydia, why our bark forsake;
The road to western deserts take?
That lip--on which hung half my bliss,
Some savage, now, will bend to kiss...

So Freneau confessed a love--and in two years he was to wed Eleanor Forman. Did he ever see Lydia Morris again? Was she the real love of his life? Men seldom marry their top choice--was his Eleanor a second or third choice? Doubtless she read this poem--was she jealous? After marriage, Freneau's relations seem to have been most perfunctory. Did the dream of the lost Lydia come between them?

Back in Monmouth that fall, Freneau continued to write essays, evidently, for the Aurora, and probably returned to Philadelphia to assist in the printing and editing. "An American" defended President Madison[31]--and the "Old Soldier" told folks that the Whigs (Democrats) were better than Federalists.[32] "Nathan," in the "Slender" style, condemned war.[33] And "Mentor" inveighed against England as worse than France.[34] All these essays repeated, in different words, the same old Freneau ideas that had so long characterized his writings.

Notes

1. New York Weekly Museum (WM), Aug. 1, 8, 1801. In 1815 Poems as "On Arriving in South Carolina, 1798." Thirteen stanzas.
2. WM, April 16, 1803. Thirteen stanzas. In 1809 Poems as "Stanzas published at the Procession to the Tomb of the Patriots..."
3. Aurora, July 28, 1801.
4. True American (TA), Aug. 18, Sept. 8, 1801.
5. Ibid., Sept. 29, Oct. 6, 1801; Feb. 23, July 19, 1802; Sept. 5, 1803.
6. Aurora, Feb. 11, 16, 23, 14, March 3, 1802.
7. Ibid., Feb. 19, 20, 1802.

8. TA, May 11, June 7, 1802. The quotation is from May 11.

9. CG, July 2, 1804. From 1815 Poems, 19 stanzas. The destruction of the town of Funchal is featured.

10. CG, July 9, 1804. From 1815 Poems as "On the Peak of Teneriffe, 1804." 6 stanzas.

11. Aurora, Sept. 3, 1804. This was a presidential year. Leary, p. 473.

12. Aurora, Sept. 6, 1804.

13. Ibid., Oct. 4, 6, 8, 1804. Leary, p. 473.

14. Aurora, The Duel, Nov. 15, 17, 21, 26, 1804. Quote is from Nov. 26.

15. Aurora, July 13, 20, Aug. 22, 30, Sept. 10, 1808.

16. Ibid., Aug. 12, 1808.

17. Ibid., Nov. 17, 1808.

18. Ibid., Nov. 19, 21, Dec. 15, 29, 30, 1808.

19. Ibid., Dec. 15, 1808.

20. Ibid., Dec. 15, 1809.

21. Ibid., Jan. 24, Feb. 1, 8, 1809.

22. Ibid., Jan. 31, 1809.

23. Ibid., Feb. 13, 15, 1809.

24. Ibid., March 22, 1809.

25. Ibid., June 22, 23, 24, 26, 27, 1809.

26. TA, March 2, 1809. Leary, p. 473. From the 1815 Poems.

27. From the 1815 Poems. 7 stanzas. Originally printed in Philadelphia in 1809, but this printing has not been found. Leary, p. 473.

28. Leary, p. 329.

29. 1809 Poems, II, 248-249.

30. He may not have intended this for publication (Leary, p. 442). But once in print, in CG (Jan. 30, 1788), he reprinted it in the 1795 Poems and in the 1809 Poems (II, 198-201), in 25 stanzas. Her name was Lydia Morris. She sailed, probably from a Jersey port, to Savannah, then left for West Georgia. She was a Quaker. Oddly, in the 1809 edition, Freneau dated it "December 30th, 1806."

31. Aurora, Sept. 27, 28, 1809. Decidedly Freneauesque.

32. Ibid., Oct. 7, 9, 1809. This a nearly sure pseudonym of Freneau.

33. Ibid., Nov. 13, 1809.

34. Ibid., Nov. 28, Dec. 12, 1809.

Chapter 7

The Last Active Years

In 1810, evidently Freneau continued to write essays for the Aurora. One comic series, poking fun at Governor Snyder in the "Slender" style, was signed "Stophel Funk."[1] Stophel, ironically charging a lie to "Conrad Weiser" (probably Duane's son, William T.), ridiculed the governor---[2]

> "Conrad Weiser"...has boldly asserted, that Simon Snyder is not qualified for the office he fills--How so? Is he not of the masculine gender, and is not a man...to be governor?... He is not like Suwarrof; he does not run about bare headed... Is not Napoleon the most extraordinary man of this or any other age? And are not the points of resemblance between him and Simon Snyder many and wonderful? Napoleon eats, and so does Simon Snyder...

I. The "Old Soldier" Essays

In November the "Old Solder," now a Freneau trade mark, raised his voice against renewing the charter of the national bank---[3]

> The directors of the United States bank now apply for a renewal of their charter.--Congress never had the right ---they never can have the right, to grant one, until the people expressly give them the dangerous prerogative--- no state in the union has a right to grant such a ruinous and destructive monopoly...

The subject was continued in 1811 under "The Bank Distemper!!" by "Sangrado," who poked fun at bookseller Mathew Carey, a prominent advocate of the bank, with the silly assumption that he must be insane.

After some months, the "Old Soldier" took up the Indian question,[5] this time with a calm, unromantic approach, quite different from the romantic idealization of the redmen in the Tomo Cheeki papers. Very likely Freneau's friend, Brackenridge, who had lived in Pittsburgh close to the savages, but visiting Philadelphia often, had convinced his old friend that, with savages, one must be realistic, and that they had no legal right to the land they occupied, and that they respected only force. And so, quite solemnly, the "Old Soldier" advised:[6]

> We are now involved in an Indian war; and had we been wise, we might have seen it long ago. The simple pass on and are punished. I am not sorry that the Indians gave the first blow, for it will embarrass the British agents in the United States, and the infamous tories... that the Indians are excited and supported by the British, no man of information will dispute...
>
> Provisions must now be made, for fresh meat is not good before harvest... Forts should be built at 25 miles distance on the road which the army is to march... All communication between Fort Malden and the Indians must be immediately stopped...

If further evidence were needed to show that Freneau was active in Philadelphia, it is provided by the publishing, in the Aurora, of another of his well-known "newsboy" poems summarizing the times and events, at New Year:[7]

> Believe us, dear patrons, we are truly sincere,
> When we tell you, we wish you a happy New Year...
>
> Thus wretchedly governed, thus robb'd and oppress'd,
> The people of England are sorely distress'd;
> And seeing their government legalize fraud,
> And robbing and piracy daily applaud,
> The example they follow, and thus have been made
> A nation of robbers and pirates by trade.
> Our vessels they capture, our seamen impress,
> And the cargoes they pocket by legal finesse,
> Take vessel and cargo and seamen by force:
> A banditti of highwaymen could not act worse...

As might be expected, the poet complains of British impressment and cargo seizure, which were soon to force President Madison to declare war.

II. The War-of-1812 Years

Now, January to October, 1812, a lapse in Freneau's publications occurred, unlike him and inexplicable. In June, President Madison, pressed by all sides (except New England) reluctantly signed a declaration of war against England. With his old friend acting thus, and entering another campaign for the presidency and becoming re-elected, why didn't Freneau speak? It remains a mystery. Perhaps he was travelling.

When he finally spoke, it was evidently through the "Old Soldier," in a "report from the West" and the Indian war there, against Tories.[8] He lectured on the unwisdom of leniency with the savages: "The Old Indian School must be Changed" was the theme of several numbers;[9] he condemned professions of friendship to the murderous red men:[10]

> In times past, when Indians have barbarously murdered our women and innocent children, we have generally solicited a treaty. After some time these savages have assembled and feasted for weeks, at our expence; in the end a treaty was made with great professions of friendship; the hatchet is finally buried, and large presents are given as evidences of our sincerity and friendship. These are deemed by the Indians as evidences that we fear them... they are a lazy, idle set of wretches... a cowardly set of villains...

The writer added that the British bribed them to kill Americans.

In December, "Hawser Trunnion," a Freneau pseudonym,[11] wrote two essays on the need of a larger navy, yet the folly of rivalling the British:[12]

> Our naval operations to be effectual must necessarily be predatory... The frigates President, United States, and Constitution, are of a class perfectly original, and decidedly superior in force, strength and velocity, to any frigates in Europe... Fleetness of sailing close-hauled, is of all other qualities the most essential to an inferior force... Sloops of war of the description of the Wasp and Hornet, are a most useful class of vessels for predatory warfare...

And once again, for the 1813 New Year, Freneau wrote a greeting for the newsboys, in it praising especially Harrison, leading the Indian war in the West:[13]

> Brave HARRISON surely must form an exception;
> On him we would certainly cast no reflection;
> He is brave, he is active, is faithful and true,
> And has done ev'ry thing that a general could do;
> To cut off the Indians, the allies of Britain,
> The best of all plans in the world he has hit on;

And no doubt will in time reduce to submission,
These engines of hell and fiends of perdition...

And through the year, it appears he wrote for the Aurora a total of twenty-two numbers, four by "Old Soldier" and four by "L." (one of his pseudonyms).[14] "L." wrote on "Internal Navigation"--[15]

> The trade on the western waters has become an object of additional importance since we have been at war with England. A steam boat of large dimensions has been running more than 12 months, between New Orleans and Natchez, another is now building at Pittsburg of 145 feet keel, to run between Natchez and the falls of the Ohio, and two others are building on the Ohio to run from the falls of that river to Pittsburg... New Orleans sugar has lately been sold at the enormous price of $25 per 112 lb.... which shall stand us no more than 15 cents per lb....

That fall "Americus" charged the Federalists with not supporting the war:[16]

> I am little acquainted with the mysteries of finance, and as "all the talents of the country are already possessed," I must be content to remain in ignorance, yet I would laugh at the fool who attempted to rob me by picking my neighbor's pocket. What a masterly stroke of policy is then exhibited "in federalists refraining from purchasing the loan from those who have already contracted for it," as thereby "the government will want the means of carrying on the war!" Yet so says Pickering...

Also a series of essays by "Agricola" discussed naval problems and British prisons;[17] and in 1814 the "Old Soldier" returned to the Aurora in twelve essays on the militia, New England's faction, Carey's Olive Branch, and a democratic bank. Carey's book was a veiled criticism of New England; the "Soldier" reviewed it with strong approval,[18] especially in condemning Boston:[19]

> Boston is represented, in the tenth chapter, as the "seat of discontent and turbulence"... Boston has acted upon the state of Massachusetts, and that state has moved two other states of New England, and thus a people, proverbially orderly and rational, have been so highly excited as to be ripe for revolution...

Meanwhile "Robert Slender" made his last appearance, in an ironic appeal "To the Members of the General Ward Committee" to choose only those already in office, for new conferees: "to elect those who hold sinecures... such as aldermen."[20]

That fall, Freneau contributed verse to the New York Columbian and the New Brunswick Fredonian, yet nothing of consequence. One poem was patriotic--oddly, he wrote few such now--"To the Squadrons on the Lakes"---[21]

> The brilliant task to you assign'd
> Asks every effort of the mind,
> And every energy, combined,
> To crush the foe.
>
> Sail where they will, you must be there;
> Lurk where they can, you will not spare
> The blast of death---but all things dare
> To bring them low...

In 1815, the "Old Soldier" wrote vigorously on wars, money, British treachery, Indians, and their lack of land rights;[22] also on lazy legislators, British and Indians, pro-British Americans, and non-supporters of the war.[23]

Soon came the long-awaited news of peace, then that of Jackson's smashing victory at New Orleans, two weeks after the treaty signing, because of the slow moving of news. Details of the victory reached the Aurora pages on February 6--it had happened in January. Rumors of peace were in the paper February 13, the confirmation on the 17th. Much celebrating followed, and a great deal of hooting at the New Englanders who had predicted defeat. Strangely, Freneau's voice was absent in all this celebration. It was not till March 30 that the "Soldier," sure the Americans had beaten England, discussed the new situation:

> The continuance of peace depends on the conduct of the United States... There is but one condition which will secure peace, and that is this: England must now see, how painful, that America is her master... We have beaten her both by sea and land...

Such an interpretation of a stalemate war indicates the "Soldier's" blindness to the truth, an inability to see that England might easily have won. But she had no wish to press a war 3,000 miles away, and was tired of struggling with Napoleon.

That fall "Shamokin," much in the "Slender" manner, defended the Aurora and discussed state politics[24] and, like "Slender," he had a neighbor to talk to. In the same issue "Sam Smort" satirized Governor Snyder in verse, "A Congratulatory Ode to the Impenetrable Idol of Corruption"---[25]

> Well, Simon, thou'st really had an easy time,
> Since tricking placed thee on the stool of state;
> Indeed, good soul, thou'rt innocent of crime;
> Like Punch, thou ne'er was known to meditate:
> But all thy movements, whether good or ill,
> Depend upon the *wires*, not on thy will...

And a series of essays by "Codrus" talked on types of government, politics, parties, and elections.[26] Parties, he said, were a sport for the few. And "A Traveller" (a Freneau pseudonym) ridiculed the ease with which candidates for the M. D. got the degree at Rutgers in New Brunswick.[27]

III. The 1815 Poems

When two tiny volumes, duodecimo, appeared in New York, in the spring of 1815--*A Collection of Poems, on American Affairs, and a Variety of Other Subjects*--it was clear that Freneau, before and after 1809, had been writing poems and saving them for this edition of one hundred thirty-seven items (three by other poets). Though on the whole the poems are reflective and philosophical, some are patriotic, including a song, "The Volunteer's March," an imitation of Burns, on Bruce's address to his army, "Scots, Wha Hae"---[28]

> Ye, whom Washington has led,
> Ye, who in his footsteps tread,
> Ye, who death nor danger dread,
> Haste to glorious victory.
>
> ...
>
> Meet the tyrants, one and all;
> Freemen stand, or freemen fall--
> At Columbia's patriot call,
> At her mandate, march away!...

This proved to be a popular song, and was often republished.

"The Capture of the Guerriere" was a poem of naval action, as were "The Battle of Stonington," "The Battle of Lake Erie," "On the Capture of the United States Frigate Essex," and a few others.

The Lake Erie-Perry story is interesting:[29]

But still, to animate his men,
From gun to gun the warrior ran
And blazed away and blazed again--
   Till Perry's ship was half a wreck:
They tore away both tack and sheet. ---
Their victory might have been complete,
Had Perry not, to shun defeat,
   In lucky moment left his deck.

Repairing to another post,
From another ship he fought their host
And soon regain'd the fortune lost,
   And down, his flag the Briton tore...

Thus, for dominion of the lake
These captains did each other rake,
And many a widow did they make;--
   Whose is the fault, or who to blame?--
The Briton challenged with his sword,
The yankee took him at his word,
With spirit laid him close on board--
   They're ours--he said--and closed the game.

The war poems are in the second volume, with other and better poems. There are tributes to Jefferson and Paine, and to Freneau's friend, Aedanus Burke of South Carolina, and a long poem, "The Tomb of the Patriots" (on the prison-ship dead). There is also a delightful comedy, "To a Caty-Did," in eight irregular stanzas:

   From your lodgings on the leaf
Did you utter joy or grief--?
Did you only mean to say,
I have had my summer's day,
And am passing, soon, away
To the grave of Caty-did:---
      Poor, unhappy Caty-did!

   But you would have utter'd more
Had you known of nature's power---
From the world when you retreat,
And a leaf's your winding sheet,
Long before your spirit fled,
Who can tell but nature said,
Live again, my Caty-did!
      Live, and chatter Caty-did.

   Tell me, what did Caty do?
Did she mean to trouble you?--
Why was Caty not forbid
To trouble little Caty-did?---
Wrong, indeed, at you to fling,

Hurting no one while you sing
Caty-did! Caty-did! Caty-did!...

This lovely poem, ignored by critics, is to be classed with "The Wild Honey Suckle" for its sympathy with nature, its pity for the ephemeral life of a humble creature, and its touch of humor.

Volume II includes "On Political Sermons," a criticism of pastors who preach politics, especially pro-British politics; "The Hypochondriac," a rebuke to complainers, suggesting that work would cure them; "Pythona, or the Prophetess of En-dor," the tale of Saul and the witch who called up from the dead Samuel, who, asked by Saul what to do, told him David would conquer and succeed him, whereupon Saul was shocked.

But the first volume is evidently where the author's real interest lay, especially in the deistic poems "On the Religion of Nature," "On Superstition," "On the Uniformity and Perfection of Nature," "On the Universality and Other Attributes of the God of Nature," "On the Evils of Human Life," and "Belief and Unbelief." "On Superstition" praises reason as a gift of God, and condemns superstition as an enemy to virtue in nine stanzas:

Here moral virtue finds its bane,
Hence, ignorance with her slavish train,
Hence, half the vigor of the mind
Relax'd, or lost in human kind.

...

The reasoning power, celestial guest,
The stamp upon the soul impress'd,
When Superstition's awe degrades,
Its beauty fails, its splendor fades.

"On the Religion of Nature" is a declaration of the deistic theory in five stanzas of the "Honey Suckle" type:

The power, that gives with liberal hand
The blessing man enjoys, while here,
And scatters through a smiling land
The abundant products of the year;
That power of nature, ever bless'd,
Bestow'd religion with the rest.

...

Religion, such as nature taught,
With all divine perfection suits:
Had all mankind this symptom sought
Sophists would cease their vain disputes,
And from this source would nations know
All that can make their heaven below...

In "Belief and Unbelief" Freneau argues that evidence is needed for real belief, discrediting mere belief, or simple faith; he defended the right to doubt in nine stanzas, four-line tetrameter stanzas:

On mere belief no merit rests,
As unbelief no guilt attests:
Belief, if not absurd and blind
Is but conviction of the mind,

Nor can conviction bind the heart
Till evidence has done its part:
And, when that evidence is clear,
Belief is just, and truth is near...

This little edition, Freneau's last, was a declaration of his artistic independence, as in "On the Abuse of Human Power, as exercised over opinion," in six stanzas:

What human power shall dare to bind
The mere opinions of the mind?
Must man at that tribunal bow
Which will no range to thought allow
But his best powers would sway or sink,
And idly tells him what to THINK...

Yet, like Pope, he defended the status quo, in six stanzas of "On the Uniformity and Perfection of Nature"---

No imperfection can be found
In all that is, above, around, --
All nature made, in reason's sight
Is order all, and _all is right._

It seems odd that these opposing views could exist together, the freedom to doubt and differ, yet the need of accepting things as they are. But we should not expect consistency from Freneau, or perhaps from any creative poet.

On the whole, the _Collection_ has variety, and an interesting, if unorthodox, grouping. Its general lack of orthodoxy probably was the strong factor in making it a sales failure. The time was no longer ripe for a Freneau. Modern, witty, sophisticated writers like Irving and Paulding were taking the public fancy. And English romantic poets, Coleridge, Wordsworth, Byron, and Scott were dominating the poetic scene, so there was little room for an old fashioned American poet. Possibly the tribute to Paine hurt him, and the fact that his printer, Longworth, was a Federalist. It was sad as he desperately needed money.

The Collection made almost no impression on the reading public; Brevoort in the Analectic Magazine may have expressed the general attitude:[30]

> Readers of a very refined taste will not, probably, relish the general style... for it is marked with a certain rusticity... that can only be palliated by the wit and humour... or the influence it may exercise in kindling patriotic and heroic feelings... Mr. Freneau has considerable merit in this way; and as he makes no high pretensions to classic grace or elevation, he should not be judged by the severe rules of criticism... we have no inclination to dwell on his defects; we had much rather
>
> With full applause, in honour to his age,
> Dismiss the veteran poet from the stage;
> Crown his last exit with distinguished praise,
> And kindly hide his baldness with the bays.
>
> B.

Later, another critic was also kind:[31]

> Nor let that "veteran poet" be forgot,
> Simple in tongue, but eloquent in thought,
> Who rose in ages, when the wheels of war
> Trod letters down beneath her fiery car:
> Let FRENEAU live! though Flattery's baleful tongue
> Too early turned his youthful lyre to song,
> And ripe old age, in ill-directed zeal,
> Has made an ennervated, last appeal:
> His song could fire the sailor on the wave,
> Raise up the coward,--animate the brave...
>
> Let the old Bard, whose patriot voice has fann'd
> The fire of Freedom that redeemed our land,
> Live on the scroll with kindred names that swell
> The page of history, where their honours dwell...

The Collection, though interesting, is, on the whole, only fairly good verse. The author had lost the fire that produced "The Power of Fancy," "The Pictures of Columbus," "The Rising Glory of America," "The Indian Burying Ground," and "The Wild Honey Suckle."

IV. The Post-War Years

Again in need--his helpful brother Peter had died two years before--evidently Freneau returned to help edit and print the Aurora, for essays of his stamp appeared in 1816. The "Old Soldier" started the year with three essays, all in January, urging the Treasury be opened to the public, that the national bank serve all the people, and condemning Gallatin's management of the Treasury Department.

Meanwhile Freneau sent an occasional essay to the Weekly Museum. One was on ladies, praising talent and intelligence in them.[32] One was titled "Lycidas," a biography;[33] and one was "On the Spots in the Sun,"[34] illustrating his interest in astronomy, and revealing his deistic interpretation of it:

> These brilliant solar orbs, the blazing suns of the firmament, like the systems of government contrived by man, seem to contain the seeds of their own dissolution. Nature will take her time; I should rather have said, the God of nature, whether to renovate, or to leave their place a blank in the creation, as best suits the will of supreme wisdom.---Intellect alone, that emanation from the Deity, is secure from the effects of these changes... and MIND... will survive when matter is no more...

Apparently he stayed in Monmouth most of the year now, contributing about a dozen poems to the Museum, inconsequential bits signed "F." or "P. F."[35] In 1817, it seems, he was again in Philadelphia. An essay by "Old Soldier" praising Joseph Reed,[36] a satire of Carey and caucuses,[37] and one aimed at William Findley by "Stench Coaxe" in the "Slender" manner[38] told that he was there. And the Museum carried a pleasant dream essay, "The River of Life," signed "L.," a Freneau pseudonym.[39] The dreamer, floating down the river of life, disembarks on the bank of pleasure; becoming bored, he rowed for the bank of wisdom, but was thrown back; trying a middle course, he found it worse. Carried to the brink of the cataract, he feared he was about to die---

> I heard a voice address me---"Thoughtless mortal! thou hast spent the day of probation--the day that departs, but does not return. With life and death before thee, thou hast chosen the latter; the votaries of folly have

> beguiled thee... Behold destruction before! Who shall struggle with these conflicting elements? Who shall survive the cataract of destruction?
>
> I started up, and heard the dashing of waters, and the shrieks of perishing wretches. The waves were already heaping around me---I was on the tremendous brink, when---I awoke, glad to find a respite from that destruction, which is not the dream of the moment, but an endless death! L.

In 1818, only one Aurora essay testifies to Freneau's writing, a satire on politicians and their ambitions, by "Momus."[40] Then tragedy struck on October 18. While the family was at church, the old home burned down, and with it many books and manuscripts. A nearby house was engaged, and in 1824 the family moved just outside Freehold, where Freneau lived till death. Two of his daughters had wed, so that the family consisted of the other two, spinsters Margaret and Mary, his wife Eleanor, and himself. The fire was a great shock to him; evidently he wrote nothing till mid-1820; at least, he published nothing known till then.

Then the "Old Soldier" returned with four essays against Findley (incumbent) and for Hiester, for governor of Pennsylvania.[41] And there came a reminder of the "Bunkers" of 1804, in a "Slenderized" essay of mock fear of a return of the Adams-type rigors, as a result of the postmaster's refusal to distribute the Aurora, signed "Joel Bunker, Jun. Son of Old Joe:"[42] both Joe and Joel had signed essays in 1804.

In 1821, "Office Hunting--a Dream," signed "Somnus," ridiculed selfish office-seekers.[43] In August of that year came another Bunker letter, by "Joe Bunker," in the "Slender" manner, criticizing John Q. Adams, then Secretary of State under Monroe, and evidently anticipating the presidency---Madison and Monroe had so become President--but Freneau disliked him and distrusted him as a former Federalist:[44]

> Mr. Duane---I am at a loss whether to attribute it to contempt, or admiration, that so little has been said or sung, of Mr. John Q. Adams' 4th July address... I was a long time diffident of making an effort to express my opinions... of that transcendant oration. General criticism, however, is not my object... Besides, sir, Mr. Adams is a great man, and I am nothing but a poor me-

> chanic!... Mr. Adams is certainly trying to appear a republican... It has astonished me, sir, that nobody should think it worth while to reflect upon Mr. Adams' sincerity, in his decorous, and creditable task of sneering at science and literature... was Mr. Adams sincere in all this abuse of English courage, letters, science, art, and all that ennobles and dignifies a nation... there is sufficient reason to believe, that he inherited a bountiful portion of prejudice in favor of England. His education was every way calculated to confirm this bias... He must be detected in INSINCERITY...
>
> Again---We ask, why never exhibit himself before? Was this the first anniversary of our freedom? No---but Mr. Adams now aspires to the presidency... I have searched in vain, sir, for some slight proof of those transcendant abilities in Mr. Adams, which should distinguish a candidate for the first office... we are not, be assured, sir, to be cajoled into the election of this official prince regent, by a fourth of July address---characterized by such a farrago of profound nonsense... such palpable hypocrisy...
>
> JOE BUNKER.

Now doubtless in painful need, the aging poet in 1822 proposed a new edition of mixed poetry and prose; but the project failed, probably for a lack of subscriptions. Thereupon Freneau contributed many new poems, and some essays, to the Trenton True American. These appeared from 1821 to 1825; many were also printed in the Fredonian of New Brunswick; some of these did not appear in the True American. Subjects were largely modern--the cession of East Florida by Spain, Napoleon at St. Helena, Jersey City, modern Greece, the Erie Canal, Princeton College, etc. Evidently he wrote the 1824 "True-American News-Boys' Annual Address," part of which has unusual merit for this usually doggerel performance. Some lines are very lyrical:[45]

> Land of the Just, the Brave, the Free,
> My heart with rapture turns to thee,
> COLUMBIA! Where the Tyrant's throne,
> Its Priests and Nobles, are unknown;
> The People hold the Sovereign sway,
> And make the laws themselves obey...

The other titles make an interesting pot-pourri:[46] "The Dotage of Royalty," "The City Poet," "The Female Astronomer," "On the Civilization of the Western Aboriginal Country," "Lines to a

Lady, Engaged in manufacturing an elegant superfine CARPET," "The Midnight Storm in the Gulph Stream," "ODE Written on a remote perspective view of PRINCETON COLLEGE," "On a Transient View of Monticello, in Virginia," "On a widow (Very rich and very penurious)," "General De La Fayette," and "On Signiora CRACHAMI, the Sicilian dwarf lady," and so on, a lively variety illustrating the genuine universality of Freneau's interests.

There is no great poetry here. Most of it is either comments on a contemporary subject, or memories out of the past, like "Stanzas Written on a visit to a field called 'THE MILITARY GROUND' near Newburgh, in the State of New-York, where the American Army were disbanded, by General WASHINGTON, almost forty years ago"---[47]

> The hills remain--but scarce a man remains
> Of all, who once paraded on these lands;
> Yet the rough soil some vestiges retains
> Of camps, and crowds, and military bands:
> I mark, I trace a spot renowned in fame,
> And something, still, may Fancy's pencil claim.
>
> . . .
>
> The vulture screams!---approaching night I see;
> This scene of soldiers soon will be concealed,
> Where once, perhaps, they met at yonder tree,
> Where once, no doubt, my friend, like us they smiled,
> To think that *George,* the terror of mankind,
> Here to another GEORGE, a world resigned!

There are several readable essays under "Recollections of Past Times and Events": one a comic dialog between a creditor and a Revolutionary debtor trying to pay a debt with depreciated currency, one about the Boston Tea Party, another about Liberty Poles and the struggle in New York to maintain a local pole against Tory attacks. One describes the Bermudians as wishing union with the United States, and includes a poem related to Shakespeare's *Tempest,* which was based on the tale of a shipwreck there:[48]

> This Island *Shakespear* made the haunt
> Of spirits from the vasty deep,
> Where PROSPER waved his magic wand
> Or in his cavern fell asleep;
> While *Calyban* contrived a plot,
> With sharpened steel, to cut his throat.

Maranda there, his daughter fair,
   Still lives in one bright nymph I see;
Her cherry lip, her auburn hair
   Might tempt one to idolatry:
And yet 'tis true, 'tis surely true,
(Revealed to me, but known to few)
She has one fault, but not first rate;
She wants Bermuda made a STATE.

...

But who comes here, approaching near,
   What blue-eyed hag, mis-shapen form?
'Tis Sycorax, by all that's good...

SYCORAX.

"From shaded cliffs and rocky reefs
I shaped my course on borrowed wings
   To fetch some dew, to fetch some due;
A sail appears on yond' deep sea
That brings some welcome news to me...

"The times arrive when I alone
   Should have these islands in my care,
But now, too old to mount a throne
   I name a Regent---'tis but fair,
And Calyban shall govern here! ...

Sept. 1778 F.

One essay tells of Freneau's visit to San Domingo, where he learned of the burial of Columbus's bones there, taken from Seville to the Cathedral of the Ozama River in the eastern end of the island, and re-discovered in 1783.[49]

Freneau also translated a fragment from the works of Bion, an ancient Greek philosopher:[50]

If God or Fate to men would give
In two succeeding States to live,
The first in pain and sorrow pass'd,
In pleasure, ease, content, the last,
I then would rack my anxious brain
With study, how that state to gain...

Commenting on the poem, Freneau said: "He believed that the soul and body died together... Yet it is remarkable, he here declares that if he could persuade himself that there was to be a future state of happiness...he would think no diligence or pains too much... What a lesson for the professors of christianity... !"

Freneau's interest in astronomy is again shown in "Contemplations, from a view of Saturn's Ring"---[51]

Lend me a wing, to waft me far
Beyond the brilliant Evening Star--
Fain would I trace the etherial way
That leads to scenes of endless day.

Where the CREATOR stands confest
In all his bright perfections dress'd--
Too bright to suit our mortal state,
And Angels, trembling, contemplate!

His last contribution to the Aurora apparently was one signed "K.," a pen-name often used by him, in 1824, "La Fayette," a review of the Memoirs of Gilbert Motier La Fayette, by H. L. Holstein, and of an article on the same subject in Biographie des Hommes Civants.[52] He pointed out errors in mistaking words and dates.

His last known publication in his lifetime is "Lines... on the Battle of Monmouth," readable but undistinguished verse in rhymed tetrameters:[53]

When orders arrived, and the battle began,
Not a musket was levelled, but brought down its man;
Not a cannon exploded, its aim was so just,
But Hessians and Britons were hurled in the dust:--
Let them sleep, let them sleep, in the fields where they bled,
'Till the lands and the ocean shall give up their dead...

FAYETTE, with the front of a lion, came on;
In the view of six thousand, his sabre was drawn;
With the stars, and the stripes, & the lillies of France,
The Royalists trembled to see him advance...

Hark! the drums how they beat, and the fifes how they play!
What a harvest of men will be cut down this day!
With the sun in the west, what a lesson it brings
To the sons of the Yankees and subjects of kings!...

Sir Harry, unwilling much longer to stay,
Press'd loyal conductors to shew them the way,
Through fields and through forests they hastened their flight,
And halted but once till the sea was in sight...

Young soldiers! may Peace be forever your lot,
But, be not the Battle of Monmouth forgot...
F.

His last known poem is "Winter," a manuscript fragment dated November 28, 1827. In it a grandfatherly poet speaks out of a nostalgic wisdom to the young in heroic couplets, thirty-two lines:[54]

The sun hangs low!---so much the worse, we say,
For *those* whose pleasure is a Summer's day;
Few *are* the Joys which stormy Nature yields
From blasting winds and desolated fields;
Their only pleasure in that season found
When orchards bloom and flowers bedeck the ground.

But, are no joys to these cold months assigned?
Has winter nothing to delight the mind?
No friendly Sun that beams a distant ray,
No social Moons that light us on our way?--
Yes, there are Joys that may all storms defy,
The chill of nature, and a frozen Sky.

Happy with wine we may indulge an hour;
The noblest beverage of the mildest power.
Happy, with Love to solace every care,
Happy with sense and wit an hour to share;
These to the mind a thousand pleasures bring
And give to winter's frosts the smiles of Spring;
Above all praise, pre-eminence they claim
Nor leave a sting behind---remorse and shame.

Ye Nymphs and Swains on Hudson's quiet shore,[55]
Blest in your *Village*, who would wish for more?
Compare your state with thousands of our kind;
How happy are you in the lot you find!---
While others shiver in the cheerless hut
And freeze o'er charcoal, or a peck of Soot,
Scarce on their beds a blanket or a sheet,
With little left to hope, and less to eat;
You sit conversing by your hickory fires,
For social purpose met, that never tires,

Contrast the Scene with Greenland's wastes of Snow
Where darkness rules and oceans cease to flow,[56]

A Valedictory from Age to Youth, "Winter" serves as a note of farewell from Freneau to the world, though probably not so intended. The old poet, we are told, continued to publish poems in the *Monmouth Enquirer.*[57]

Notes

1. *Aurora,* Jan. 20, 25, 27, Feb. 1, 6, 8, 15, 1810.
2. *Ibid.*, Jan. 15, 1810.
3. *Ibid.*, Nov. 29, 1810.
4. *Ibid.*, Jan. 18, 22, 28, Feb. 14, 23, 1811. Very probably by Freneau.
5. *Ibid.*, Dec. 12, 19, 20, 1811; Jan. 1, 18, 1812.
6. *Ibid.*, Dec. 30, 1811.

7. Ibid., Jan. 1, 1812. Issued also as a broadside. At the Pennsylvania Historical Society.
8. Ibid., Oct. 21, 1812.
9. Ibid., Nov. 14, 24, Dec. 9, 14, 1812.
10. Ibid., Nov. 24, 1812.
11. Freneau used it in FJ, Aug. 28, 1782. Leary, p. 474.
12. Aurora, Dec. 22, 1812. Also on Dec. 24, 1812.
13. Ibid., Jan. 1, 1813, with a separate broadside.
14. "L." was recognized by Leary as Freneau; see pp. 211-212, in an editorial.
15. Aurora, July 3, 1813.
16. Ibid., Oct. 26, 1813. Other essays by "Americus" came out Oct. 20 and Nov. 13, 1813, probably by Freneau. Pickering, formerly Secretary of War and of State, was now a representative from Massachusetts.
17. Ibid., Nov. 10, Dec. 16, 17, 29, 1813.
18. Ibid., Nov. 19, 22, 24, 25, 26, 1814.
19. Ibid., Nov. 25, 1814. The semi-revolutionary Hartford Convention met Dec. 15 to Jan. 5, 1814-15.
20. Ibid., Aug. 25, 1814. Leary (p. 474) has it the 11th.
21. Columbian, Sept. 29, 1814. From 1815 Poems. 10 stanzas.
22. Aurora, Jan. 2, 11, 15, 1815.
23. Ibid., Feb. 2, 3, March 30, July 10, Aug. 25, 1815.
24. Ibid., Oct. 9, 1815.
25. Ibid., three stanzas. Probably by Freneau.
26. Ibid., Oct. 13, 16, 18, 25, 1815. Freneau's, probably.
27. Ibid., Nov. 2, 1815.
28. First published in the Fredonian (New Brunswick, N. J.), Aug. 11, 1814. Leary, p. 474. 8 stanzas.
29. In 1815 Poems, II, 105-108. 10 stanzas.
30. June, 1815. Leary (pp. 340-341) assumed the review was by Verplanck. But it was signed "B." Irving was the editor; and Henry Brevoort, his friend, was writing for the magazine. Verplanck signed with "V." See S. T. Williams, The Life of Washington Irving, New York, 1935, I, 138.
31. Trenton True American (TA), Oct. 7, 1820. From Robert Waln, American Bards, Philadelphia, 1820.
32. WM, March 5, 1814. Signed "F."
33. Ibid., March 23, 1816. Signed "F."

34. Ibid., Sept. 7, 1816. Signed "P. F." "Solar Spots" appeared in the Aurora of June 21, 1816, signed "Z."--a Freneau pseudonym.

35. Leary, pp. 475-476. Leary lists nothing written by Freneau from late 1816 to mid-1821.

36. Aurora, July 18, 1817. Reed, once president of Pennsylvania, was idealized by Freneau.

37. Ibid., by "Circumbendibus."

38. Ibid., Sept. 23, 1817.

39. WM, Sept. 20, 1817.

40. Aurora, Aug. 26, 1818.

41. Ibid., July 11, 20, Aug. 9, 24, 1820.

42. Ibid., Dec. 5, 1820.

43. Ibid., Feb. 20, 1821. By Freneau, probably.

44. Ibid., Aug. 30, 1821. The close: "I am, Mr. Duane, your old friend."

45. TA, Jan. 3, 1824.

46. Leary, in The Last Poems of Philip Freneau, New Brunswick, N. J., 1945, page xi, identified most of these poems by their signatures--letters from FRENEAU.

47. TA, June 8, 1822. 6 stanzas.

48. TA, Aug. 10, 1822. Freneau, it seems, fell in love with a Bermuda girl, a daughter of the governor. 8 irregular stanzas.

49. TA, Aug. 17, 1822. Unsigned, but with "Recollections No. 4."

50. TA, Nov. 23, 1822.

51. TA, Feb. 5, 1825. Unsigned, but doubtless Freneau's.

52. Aurora, Sept. 15, 1824.

53. TA, June 30, 1827. 138 lines, signed "F." Not in Leary.

54. Manuscript at the New York Public Library.

55. The poem was probably addressed to Freneau's grandchildren, who lived in Newburgh, on the Hudson River.

56. End of manuscript.

57. Leary, pp. 363, 408.

Chapter 8

Critical Conclusions

In his declining years, Freneau turned again to poetry as his chief manner of expression, and largely abandoned prose. Yet his later essays are better prose than his last poems are poetry. Somewhere in the controversies of the 1790's his at-times-delicate poetic genius had been blunted. He never wrote again as he had written occasionally before 1790. His essays developed power as journalism, as a political weapon, and as entertainment; but they were not literary.

As a whole, however, from 1768 to 1827, he had created an astounding volume of writings, ranging in subjects from insects and flowers to astronomy and deism, more variety than any other early American writer had created; and more than any one of his contemporaries, he experimented with forms: in poetic forms, both stanzas and lines; and in prose, the Addisonian essay, the ironic satire, even some fiction. In verse, he favored the heroic couplet, the Gray stanza, and the "Honey Suckle" grouping of six lines: tetrameter, ababcc. He aimed at an epic, but fell short, yet wrote several items in the epic manner. He tried a play, but never finished it. One form he never tried was the novel.

His main literary inspirations seem to have been Homer, Virgil, Horace, Shakespeare, Dryden, Pope, Swift, Gray, Addison, and Goldsmith. He admired Shakespeare's work most; in prose it was Addison; he used the dramatic form a great deal, and often wrote essays along the Addison line. In "Eutaw Springs," evidently he imitated Collins's "Ode Written in the Beginning of the Year 1746." He imitated Burns in "The Volunteers' March." Like Shakespeare, he was both imitator and originator. In nature poems, he was a precursor of Wordsworth and Bryant, and probably influenced Wordsworth and Coleridge.

He would write on any subject that stirred up an interest,

often on current events. But his main interests were Britain, Tories, Federalists, France, monarchy, democracy, and Indians. One fault was putting into verse his feuds with rival editors like Fenno and Webster. Yet he would create, almost carelessly, a lasting poem like "The Power of Fancy" or "The Wild Honey Suckle," or a purely romantic essay like the best in Tomo Cheeki. Thus we find not only a great range of subject matter; there is also a great range of styles and quality, from bad to the best, with a few gems that should live in American literature, perhaps forever.

Freneau's repute would have fared better since his death had he not become known as a defender of Paine and Revolutionary France, and as a satirist of Washington, Adams, and Hamilton, who were nearly sainted by historians and biographers in the nineteenth and early twentieth centuries. In recent years, however, realistic appraisals of all three, especially of Hamilton, have removed part of the halos that glorified them. And biographies of Jefferson, Madison, Monroe, and Freneau have revealed them as better than had been thought. This is especially true of Jefferson, once supposed to be an arch-villain behind all the opposition to Washington, and the secret editor of the National Gazette.

Freneau, pictured as the servile tool of the great but crafty Democrat, now is emerging in a better light as a really independent editor, and even more of a "radical" than Jefferson was.

With all his faults, Philip Freneau was a sincere idealist, a devotee (often rabid) of real democracy, an intense hater of all tyranny and aristocracy (including monarchy); and he lived a life in some ways truly heroic. He dreamed of the highest ideals, thought they should be realized or enforced in the present, lived close to Glory, and breathed deeply, intoxicatingly, of her heavenly music. He was gripped strongly, till he was drunk with her spirit, and fired all his life with a persistent enthusiasm to sing her songs and a caustic contempt for those who would not do so. He died still hearing her clarion tones.

Guide to Notes and References

A	Argus, New York
Aurora	Philadelphia
CG	City Gazette, Charleston
DA	Daily Advertiser, New York
FJ	Freeman's Journal, Philadelphia
GUS	Gazette of the United States, Philadelphia
JC	Jersey Chronicle, Monmouth, N. J.
Leary	That Rascal Freneau, New Brunswick, N. J., 1941.
MA	Monmouth Almanac for 1795, Monmouth, N. J.
MW	Miscellaneous Works (by Freneau), Philadelphia
NG	National Gazette, Philadelphia
NJG	New Jersey Gazette, Trenton
NYJ	New York Journal
Pattee	Poems of Philip Freneau, Princeton, 1902-1907.
TA	True American, Trenton
TP	Time Piece, New York
USM	United States Magazine, Philadelphia
WM	New York Weekly Museum

Selected Bibliography
(Chronological)

PRIMARY SOURCES

New Travels Through North-America, by Claude Robin, translated by Philip Freneau. 13 essays commenting on the new republic. Philadelphia, 1783; Boston, 1784.

The Poems of Philip Freneau, Philadelphia, 1786. Freneau's first volume of poems. Contains his early poems, college and patriotic satires, the long forms of "The House of Night" and "The Beauties of Santa Cruz."

The Miscellaneous Works of Mr. Philip Freneau (MW), Philadelphia, 1788. Half poems and half prose. Contains the best lyrics--"The Wild Honey Suckle" and "The Indian Burying Ground." Also, some excellent essays.

The Monmouth Almanac for 1795, Middletown-Point (Monmouth), N. J. With fifteen essays on a wide variety of subjects.

Poems Written between the Years 1768 & 1794, Monmouth, N. J., 1795. The only volume printed by the author, and rather poorly done.

Letters... By Robert Slender, Philadelphia, 1799. Facsimile edition, Harry Clark, ed., New York, 1943. Twenty-four political essays.

Poems Written and Published during the American Revolutionary War... with Translations from the Ancients, and Other Pieces Not Heretofore in Print, Philadelphia, 1809. Two volumes, with two engraved frontispieces. Freneau's most elaborate edition.

A Collection of Poems... Written between the Year 1797 and the Present Time, New York, 1815. Two volumes. Few patriotic poems. Several deistic poems. Freneau's most mature poetry.

Newspapers and Magazines

United States Magazine, Hugh Brackenridge, ed., Philadelphia, 1779 (USM). Monthly, twelve issues, January-December. A brave attempt at creating a literary magazine in non-literary America.

The Freeman's Journal, Francis Bailey, ed., Philadelphia, 1781-1789 (FJ). Freneau helped edit this weekly newspaper for one year, and contributed to it for about ten years. A liberal Whig paper.

The Daily Advertiser, Francis Childs and John Swaine, publishers, New York, 1790-1791. DA. Neutral, politically. One of the earliest daily papers in New York. Very commercial, many advertisements.

Gazette of the United States, John Fenno, ed., New York and Philadelphia, 1789-1800. GUS. Strongly Federalist, Hamilton-dominated, cautious and conservative.

National Gazette, Philip Freneau, ed., Philadelphia, 1791-1793. NG. Strongly Republican (Democratic), critical of Federalists and Britain, pro-France. Very few advertisements.

Aurora (originally The General Advertiser, but from 1794 on known as "the Aurora" by the use of that word in the center of the title), Benjamin F. Bache, ed., 1790-98; William Duane, ed., mostly, 1798-1824, Philadelphia, 1791-1824. At first rather conservative, then Republican and very critical of Federalists; finally radically Democratic.

Jersey Chronicle, Philip Freneau, editor-publisher-printer, Monmouth, N.J., 1795-1796. JC. Democratic and international in attitude, but without influence. A rural paper, probably with very small circulation.

The Time Piece, Philip Freneau, ed., co-publisher with Alexander Menut, then Matthew Davis, 1797-98. TP. At first literary and non-political, then strongly Democratic and pro-France, anti-Adams.

The True American, James Wilson, ed., Trenton, 1801-1803, 1820-1824, 1827. TA. Strongly Democratic, liberal newspaper.

The New-York Weekly Museum, James Oram, ed., New York, 1801-17. WM. Mostly literary, with some news.

SECONDARY SOURCES

Collections

The Poems of Philip Freneau, Fred L. Pattee, ed., Princeton, 1902-1907. Pattee. Not all-inclusive, but useful despite some errors. Interesting life of Freneau in Vol. I. 3 vols.

Last Poems of Philip Freneau, Lewis Leary, ed., New Brunswick, 1945. 136 pages. Poems from WM, TA, and the Fredonian

(Fredonia, N. J.), 1816-1824, and "Winter," ms. poem of 1827. Mostly identified by signatures from the letters of FRENEAU.

The Prose of Philip Freneau, Philip M. Marsh, ed., Metuchen, N. J., 1955. Selections of prose, certain and probable--about 170 essays, mostly republished for the first time. 608 pages.

A Freneau Sampler, Philip M. Marsh, ed., Metuchen, N. J., 1963. 406 pages. A "miscellaneous works" of Freneau--selections of representative poems and essays, annotated.

Bibliographies

Victor H. Paltsits, A Bibliography of the Separate and Collected Works of Philip Freneau, New York, 1903. Reliable--but does nothing with the individual poems and essays.

Lewis Leary, That Rascal Freneau, New Brunswick, 1941. Bibliography, pages 418-420, tries to be complete, but is lacking especially in the prose. In the poetry, it is very good.

Owen P. Thomas, "Philip Freneau: A Bibliography," Proceedings of the NJHS, July, 1957. A list of items about Freneau. Useful.

Philip M. Marsh, Freneau's Published Prose: A Bibliography. To be published by the New Jersey Historical Society. Over 1100 items--certain and probable.

Biographies

Evert A. and George L. Duyckinck, Cyclopaedia of American Literature, New York, 1855. 2 vols. See I, 327-48. Interesting description of Freneau in his old age by a friend, Dr. John Francis.

Mary Austin, Philip Freneau, Poet of the Revolution, New York, 1901. Unscholarly and unreliable--but contains some letters and interesting rumors.

Fred L. Pattee, Poems of Philip Freneau (see collections), I, xiii-cxii, "Life of Philip Freneau." Interesting, though incomplete.

Lewis Leary, That Rascal Freneau, New Brunswick, 1941. Leary. Elaborate notes and large, detailed bibliography. The only scholarly biography of Freneau. Readable, but full of small errors.

Philip M. Marsh, The Prose of Philip Freneau (see collections), "Introduction." Brief discussion of Freneau's life and works.

Critical Essays

Harry H. Clark, "The Literary Influences of Philip Freneau," Studies in Philology, January, 1925. Interesting survey of poetic influences; does nothing with the prose.

---- ----, "Introduction," Poems of Freneau, New York, 1929. Interesting, but based on limited knowledge; some mistakes of assumption; biased.

Frank Smith, "Philip Freneau and The Time-Piece and Literary Companion," American Literature, November, 1932. Good analysis, good reading.

Philip M. Marsh, "Freneau and Jefferson," American Literature, May, 1936. Review of relations of Freneau and Jefferson in 1791-93.

---- ----, Monroe's Defense of Jefferson and Freneau against Hamilton, Oxford, Ohio, 1948. Six essays identified as Monroe's and republished, one about Freneau, with Hamilton's accusations. 1792-93.

---- ----, "Philip Freneau's Fame," Proceedings of the NJHS, April, July, 1962. Review of essays and comments about Freneau and his work from the 1780's to the present day.

Lewis Leary, "Philip Freneau in Charleston," The South Carolina Historical and Genealogical Magazine, July, 1941. Review of Freneau's poems in Charleston newspapers.

Index

"Academy of Death" 47
"Account of a Cave" 30
Adams, Abigail 135
Adams, John 11, 13, 17, 18, 66, 67, 86, 98, 117, 118, 120, 124, 125, 126, 129, 130, 131, 133, 136, 137, 140, 148
Adams, John Q. 66, 173
Addison, Joseph 20, 21, 39, 44, 47, 53, 102, 181, 182
"Address to my Old Hat" 68
Address to the Citizens of Holland" 71
Advertisement Extraordinary" 144
"Advice to Ladies not to Neglect the Dentist" 78
Age of Reason 157
Alexander 48
Almanac 12, 96
"America Independent" 45
American Bards 179
American Daily Advertiser 82
American Demosthenes 147
American Liberty 26
American Magazine 44
"American Village" 25, 34
"An Author's Soliloquy" 51
Analectic Magazine 171
Anas 79
André, Major 36
Argus 111, 129, 130, 149, 150
Aristippus 73
Aristotle 48
Arnold, Benedict 37
Aurora (newspaper) 13, 18, 99, 108, 111, 125, 129, 130, 131, 132, 133, 137, 138, 144, 146, 150, 155, 156, 160, 162, 163, 165, 166, 167, 172, 173, 177
Aurora (ship) 16, 36, 37

Bache, B. F. 18, 99, 111, 131, 149
Bache, Mrs. 131
Bailey, Francis 16, 36, 38, 44, 45, 46
Bailey, Lydia 155
"Balloons" 158
"Bank Distemper" 162
Barlow, Joel 63, 122
Bartram, William 106, 145
"Bastile" 60
"Battle of Lake Erie" 167
"Battle of Monmouth" 10, 109
"Battle of Stonington" 167
"Beauties of Santa Cruz 13, 30, 45, 147, 158
Beckley, John 17
"Belief and Unbelief" 169, 170
Behn, Aphra 145
"Bermuda" 116
Biddle, Charles 46
Biographie des Hommes Civants 177
Bion 176
Blair 58
Blanchard, James 75, 93, 142
Bompard, Capt. 76
Book of Odes 122
Boswell 117
Brackenridge, Hugh 16, 19, 21, 23, 28, 30, 46, 132, 145, 162
Brevoort, Henry 171, 179
"Brief Account of the Ugly Club" 59
"Brissot" 189
Britain 17, 18, 23, 26, 28, 33, 34, 45, 78, 83, 88, 110, 115, 118, 120, 130, 131, 133, 156, 159, 181
British Prison Ship 36, 45, 99, 158
Bruce, Robert 167
Bryant, William 13, 181
Bunkers 18, 154, 155, 173
Burgoyne, Gen. 28
Burk, John 129
Burke, Aedanus 46, 168
Burke, Edmund 65

Burns, Robert 167, 181
Burr, Aaron 137, 155
Byron, George 171

Cain 27
Campbell, Thomas 55
"Cantos from a Prison-Ship" 99
Captain Dauntless 54
"Capture of the Guerriere" 167
"Capture of the United States Frigate Essex" 167
Carey, Matthew 44, 46, 162, 165
Carroll, James 46
Carver 145
Cat-Island 85
"Characteristic Sketch..." 57
Childs, Francis 11, 12, 16, 17, 66, 93
Churchill, Charles 140
"Citizen's Resolve" 20, 22
City Gazette 11, 44, 53, 54, 135
"City Poet 174
Clinton, DeWitt 46, 111
Clinton, George 86
Clinton, Henry 29
Cobbett, William 120, 121, 148
Colden, Cadwallader 145
Coleridge 145, 171
Collection of Poems... 1815 167, 170, 171
Collins 181
Columbiad 125
Columbian 166
Columbian Herald 11, 44, 52
Columbus, 176
"Columbus to Ferdinand" 22
Conquest of Canaan 162
Constitutional Gazette 28
"Containing certain Indian Notions..." 103
"Contemplations from... Saturn's Ring" 176-7
Cooper, Thomas 27
"Country Printer" 70, 148
Courtney, Capt. 76
Coxe, Tench 18, 154, 155
"Crisis" 129
"Crispin O'Connor, Esq..." 73
"Curious Dialogue" 73

Daily Advertiser 11, 16, 44, 53, 54, 56, 58, 59, 63, 66, 68, 81, 98, 103, 139, 140
Darwin, Charles 119
Davila 66
Davis, Matthew 17, 119, 129
Dayton, Jonathan 151
Deane, Silas 43
"Death of a Republican Printer" 142
Decker, balloonist 91
De Coverley, Roger 39
Defoe 20
De Lahontan 145
Deism 18, 103
"Description of Connecticut" 57
"Description of New York one hundred fifty years hence" 59
"Description of Pennsylvania" 57
"Descriptive Sketch of Maryland 57
"Descriptive Sketch of Virginia" 57
"Deserted Village" 25, 70
"Detached Observations 118
"Detached Observations and Reflections" 124
"Detached reflections from a correspondent" 85
"Dialogue between a Citizen & Philadelphia... 94
"Dialogue between George and Fox" 158
"Dialogue between his Britannic Majesty and Mr. Fox" 33
"Dialogue between Satan and Arnold" 36
Dialogues Curieux 145
"Directions for Courtship" 49
"Discourse on Esquires" 47
"Discourse upon Barbers' Poles" 61
"Discourse upon Horse Shoes" 61
"Distrest Theatre" 158
Domitian 27
Doria, Andrea 126
"Dotage of Royalty" 179
"Drunkard's Apology" 66
"Drunken Soldier" 11
Dryden 20, 181
Duane, William 13, 18, 131, 133, 135, 136, 153, 154, 155
Duane, William T. 162
Duer, William 70

Dwight, Timothy 62, 63, 126, 140
"Dying Elm" 31
"Dying Indian" 145

Echo 70
"Elegy on the Death of a Blacksmith" 76
Embargo Act 18
England 15, 28, 61, 99, 156
"English Quixote of 1778, or, Modern Idolatry" 38
"Epistle from Peter Pindar" 69
"Epistle to Peter Pindar, Esq." 58
"Epitaph" 132
"Epitaph Intended for the Tombstone of Patrick Bay" 20, 22
"Epitaph on Mrs. H. Rittenhouse" 134
Epitaph to "Jonathan Robbins" 135-6
"Essay on Beauty" 114
Essays on Davila 199
"Equestrian Exercises at Mr. Rickett's Circus" 114
"Eutaw Springs" 13, 38, 45, 158, 181
"Extempore, on his excellency, the governor of Pennsylvania ..." 138

"Fancy's Ramble" 158
"Farewell to New-York" 59
"Father Dobbin's Complaint" 11
Federalists 56, 70, 74, 77, 78, 83, 98, 117, 129, 135, 138, 153, 156, 160, 165, 181
"Female Astronomer" 174
Fenno, John 11, 16, 66, 82, 98, 99, 111, 117, 120, 125, 127, 130, 131, 132, 140, 143, 154, 182
Ferdinand 51
Findley, William 172
First Chapter of the Third Book of Chronicles" 124
Flatbush 25
Forman, Eleanor 16, 54 160, 173
"Forsaken Lover" 30, 33
"Fourth of July - An Ode" 150
France 12, 17, 19, 23, 67, 78, 88, 90, 99, 113, 114, 115, 116, 117, 120, 125, 129, 130, 131, 133, 134, 182
Franklin, Benjamin 14, 39, 57, 58, 83, 137
Fredonian 166, 174
Freeman's Journal 11, 16, 38, 43, 44, 53, 68
French Revolution 60, 65, 72
French Traveller's Journal 118
Freneau, Margaret 173
Freneau, Mary 173
Freneau, Peter 16, 44, 46, 129, 152, 153, 171
Freneau, Philip, chronology 7-10, fame 11-13, biography 13-19
Freneau Sampler 19
Fresneau, Pierre 15
From the Archives of the city of Barrataria, 1693, 94
Funchal 101

Gage 26, 27, 28
Gaine, Hugh 45
Gallatin 171
Gates, Gen. 28
Gazette Nationale 118
Gazette of the United States 11, 16, 66, 78, 82, 118, 131, 132, 140
"General De La Fayette" 175
"General Gage's Confession" 27
"General Gage's Soliloquy" 27, 158
Genesis 24
Genet, Edmond 17, 88, 89, 90, 93, 99
Genoa 126
George III, 26 27, 31, 33, 34, 156
Goldsmith, Oliver 25, 26, 39, 70, 181
Gray 20, 22, 28, 30, 31, 32, 57, 121, 181
"Great Dismal" 60
Greenleaf, Thomas 111

Hamilton, Alexander 11, 12, 16, 56, 63, 73, 74, 78, 83, 88, 98, 108, 111, 117, 131, 138, 155, 157, 182
Hanson, John 15
"Happy Farmer" 59

Harrison 164
"Hatteras Shoals" 80
Hazard, Ebenezer 46
Helen of Troy 48
Herod 27
"Heroic Tale" 68
"Heroine of the Revolution" 149
Herschel, William 143
Hiester, 173
"Hint to the Public" 60
History of the Five Indian Nations 145
Homer 20, 23, 24, 48, 181
Hopkinson, Francis 14, 43, 142
Horace 20, 24, 181
"House of Night" 30, 32, 45, 99
Howe, Gen. 28
"Hugh Gaine's Life" 38-9, 158
Humphreys, David 63, 64
Hunter, ship 36
"Hurricane" 158
"Hypochondriac" 169

"Independence" 73
"Indian Burying Ground" 13, 44, 53, 99, 101, 158, 171
"Indian Convert" 149
"Interest of the Northern and Southern States forever inseparable" 78
"Internal Navigation" 165
Irving, Washington 171, 179
Isabella 51

Jackson, Andrew 166
"Jamaica Funeral" 29
Jay Treaty 100, 108, 111
"Jefferson and Liberty" 137
Jefferson, Thomas 11, 12, 16, 17, 18, 56, 63, 65, 66, 73, 78, 111, 129, 130, 137, 138, 143, 154, 155, 156, 157, 168, 182
Jersey Chronicle 12, 17, 95, 99, 101, 102, 108, 109, 110, 111, 142
"Jersey-Coast Inlets" 94
"Jewish Tradition" 109
Johnson, Samuel 140
"Journey from Philadelphia to New-York" 53
"Jug of Rum" 11, 64, 79

King's College (Columbia) 27
"King George the Third's Soliloquy" 31
"King George the Third's Speech to Lord North" 31
King of France 28
Knox, Henry 56

"La Fayette" 177
"L'Allegro" 22
"Landlord's Soliloquy" 65, 81
Last Poems of Philip Freneau 80
"Last Will and Testament of a Democrat. . ." 130
Leary 19, 33, 36, 52, 54, 55, 78, 127, 139-44, 147, 148, 150, 161, 179, 180
Lee, Charles 109
Leib, Michael 154
Letters. . . of Robert Slender 18, 133, 136, 137, 150, 151, 153
Libraries consulted v
Life and Works of Francis Hopkinson 142
Life of Samuel Johnson 117
Life of Washington Irving 179
"Light, Summer Reading" 17, 53
"Lines Addressed to a dull Country Parson" 58
"Lines Addressed to a very little man. . ." 77
"Lines Addressed to Mr. Jefferson. . ." 156
"Lines extempore on the spur of the Occasion" 135
"Lines. . . on the Battle of Monmouth" 177
"Lines occasioned by reading Mr. Paine's Rights of Man" 65
"Lines to a Lady. . ." 175
"Lines. . . to. . . Charles Lee" 109
"Lines. . . to Miss---. . ." 53
"Lines Written at Port-Royal" 53
"Lines Written for Mr. Ricketts" 147
"Lines Written. . . from New-York to. . . Madeira. . ." 114
"Lines written several years ago" 110
L'Ingenu 145
"Literary Importation" 158

Livingston, Edward 46
Lloyd 30
Logan, George 17, 46, 130
"Lost Louisa" 13, 121
Louis XIV 87
Louis XVI 88
"Loyalists" 32
"Lycidas" 172

"Mac Swiggen: a Satire" 28
Madison, James 11, 12, 13, 16, 17, 63, 129, 156, 158, 162, 163, 173, 182
Margarot 127
Markoe, Peter 46
"Mars and Hymen" 38
"Matrimonial Dialogue" 141
"Maxims and Observation" 108
McGillivray, Alexander 61
McKean, Joseph 137, 155
"Means for the Preservation of Public Liberty" 117
"Melancholy reflections... 120
Memoirs of Gilbert Motier La Fayette 177
Menut, Alexander 17, 111, 119
"Midnight Consultations..." 158
"Midnight Storm..." 175
Milton, John 20, 21, 22, 23
Minerva 119, 120
"Minerva's Advice" 66
Mirabeau 118
Miscellaneous Essays and Occasional Writings of Hopkinson 142
Miscellaneous Works, of Freneau, 5, 11, 16, 44, 46-54, 132, 159
Miscellanies for Sentimentalists 27
"Miserable Life of a Pedagogue" 26
Monmouth Almanac 96, 98, 139, 144
Monmouth Enquirer 178
"Monmouth Gazette..." 96
Monroe, James 11, 17, 117, 118, 173, 182
Montaigne 145
"Monument of Phaon" 20, 22
Morris, Lydia 160
Mount Pleasant 19
"Napoleon" 162
National Gazette 12, 16, 17, 18, 68-9, 73, 77, 78, 82, 85, 93, 95, 98, 111, 120, 139, 182
"Nereus and Thetis" 147
Nero 27
"New Liberty Pole - Take Care" 28
New Jersey Gazette 36
"New Song" 75
New-York Journal 66, 75, 111, 142, 149
"New-York Tory's Epistle" 39
New York Weekly Museum 152, 171, 172
"New Year's Verses" 44, 45
North, Lord 33, 34
Nouveau Voyage dans les Etats Unis 89

"Observations on Monarchy" 101
"Observations on the Treaty..." 160
"Ode" 117
"Ode for the Fourth of July, 1797" 147
"Ode for July the Fourth--1799" 147
"Ode to Friendship" 114
"Ode to Liberty" 75
"Ode to the Echo Writer" 70
"Ode... on... Princeton College" 175
"Ode Written on the Beginning of the Year 1746" 181
Odell 43
"Of the Planetary System" 96
Oglethorpe, Gen. 145
"Old Connecticut Blue Laws..." 119
"Old Heathen Story" 73
"Old Indian School..." 164
"Old Soldier and his Dog" 60
Olive Branch 165
"On a Bee Drinking from a Glass of Wine" 119
"On a Celebrated Performer..." 147
"On a Fly..." 127
"On a late memorable naval en-

gagement" 76
"On a Nocturnal View of the Planet Jupiter" 151
"On a View of the Planet Jupiter ..." 135
"On a Transient View of Monticello..." 175
"On a Widow..." 175
"On Arriving in South Carolina, 1798" 160
"On City Burying Places" 49
"On Deborah Gannett" 127
"On Dogs" 96, 97
"On Dr. Sangrado's Flight" 142
"On Epic Poetry" 62
"On False Systems of Government..." 148
"On Hearing a Political Oration" 147
"On hearing a remarkably dull discourse..." 115
On Imprisonment for Debt 127
"On Law" 98
"On Mr. Paine's Rights of Man" 158
"On Monarchy" 100
"On Notions" 67, 68
"On Passing by..."148
"On Pest-Eli-Hali..." 141
"On Political Sermons" 169
"On Signiora Crachami..." 175
"On some of the Principles of American Republicanism" 108
"On superstition" 169
"On the Abuse of Human Power ..." 170
"On the Approaching Dissolution of Transatlantic Jurisdiction in America" 100, 158
"On the Causes of Political Degeneracy in America" 130
"On the Civilization of the Western Aboriginal Country" 174
"On the Death of Benjamin Franklin" 158
"On the Death of Capt. N. Biddle" 36
"On the Demolition of the French Monarchy" 142
"On the Departure of the Grand Sanhedrin" 58
"On the Evils of Human Life" 169
"On the Fall of Gen. Earl Cornwallis" 158
"On the Federal City" 122
"On the Free Use of the Lancet" 148
"On the Folly of Writing Poetry" 151
"On the Fourteenth of July" 72
"On the French Republicans" 141
"On the Indian War" 85
"On the ingratitude of Republics" 108
"On the Invasion of Rome, in 1796" 147
"On the morality of commerce" 147
"On the Origin of Nobility" 79
"On the Proposed American Negociation..." 116
"On the Prospect of War..." 150
"On the Religion of Nature" 169
"On the Royal Coalition against Republican Liberty" 145
"On the Spots in the Sun" 171
"On the too Remote Extension of American Commerce" 112
"On the Uniformity and Perfection of Nature" 169, 170
"On the Universality... of the God of Nature" 169
"On the War... with... France" 147
"Opay Mico" 60, 61, 103
"Orator Skip's Apology 59
"Origin of Wars" 159
Oroonoko 145
Ossian 116

Paine, Thomas, 65-6, 137, 157, 168, 171, 182
Palmer 127
Paradise Lost 22, 23
"Parody, on the attempt to Force the British Treaty..." 109
"Particulars relative to the Bastille of France" 96
"Parting Glass" 66
"Pasquin" 138
"Patriotic Stanzas on the... Bastille" 76
Pattee 33, 34, 38, 39
Paulding 171
"Pennsylvania" 158
"People's Friend" 138

"Peter Pindar" 58
"Philosopher of the Forest" 46-7
"Philosophical Speculation" 97
Pickering, Thomas 151
"Pictures of Columbus" 50, 158, 171
"Pilgrim" 39, 46
Pinckney, Charles 46
Pintard, John 46
Pitt, Wm., 43
Plato 47
"Poem on the memorable victory..." 38
"Poem on the Rising Glory of America" 23
Poems of 1786, 11, 16, 20, 23, 27-9, 31-2, 36, 38, 48-55, 159
Poems of 1795, 12, 17, 32, 38, 96, 98, 139-42, 144, 158, 159, 161
Poems of 1809, 13, 18, 38, 122, 147-8, 150, 158
Poems of 1815, 13, 18, 122, 129, 147, 148, 150, 161, 179
"Poetical Address to the Public ..." 69
"Poetical History of the Prophet Jonah" 20
"Political Balance" 45
"Political Creed" 108
"Political Observations" 123
"Political Reflections" 134
"Pomposo" 140
"Pomposo and his Printer" 66
Pope, Alexander 20, 181
Porcupine's Gazette 120, 132
"Power of Fancy" 13, 20, 21, 23, 45, 171, 182
"Prefatory Lines to a Periodical Publication" 147
"Present Situation... in North America" 26
"Present Views of France..." 74
Princeton College 15, 20, 21
Probationary Odes... 77, 142
Proclamation of Neutrality 17, 89, 90
"Progress of Balloons" 39
"Prophecy of King Tammany" 158
"Prophet Jonah" 22
Prose of Philip Freneau 19
"Prudent Philosopher" 70
"Psalm. cxxxvii. Imitated" 33, 35
"Publius to Pollia" 147
"Pyramid of the Fifteen American States" 74
"Pyramids of Egypt" 20, 21
"Pythona..." 169

"Quintilian to Lycidas" 77

Ramsay, David 46
Randolph, Edmund 56, 108
"Receipt to make an Echo Writer" 70
"Recollections of Past Times and Events" 175
Reed, Joseph 72, 89, 180
"Reflections" 93, 110, 131
"Reflections on my first entering the great City..." 102
"Reflections on my Journey... 61
"Reflections on several subjects" 93
"Reflections on the death of a country printer" 75
"Reflections on the General Debased Condition of Mankind" 121-2
"Reflections on the Gradual Progress of Nations..." 150
"Reflections on the Recent Conduct of the king..." 150
"Reflections on walking on... Long-Island..." 152
"Register of the Times" 109, 111
"Removal" 58
"Report of a Law Case" 46-7
"Republic and Liberty" 130
"Republican Festival" 148
"Republican Genius of Europe" 101, 109
"Republican Liberties and Tendencies to Monarchy" 108
Revolution, American 32
Ridgway Library 27
"Ridiculous Distress..." 21
Rights of Man 65, 66, 142, 157
"Rising Glory of America" 14, 21, 23, 26, 45, 58
Rittenhouse, David 46
"Rival Suitors for America" 110
"River of Life" 172
Rivington 43, 45, 46

"Rivington's Confession" 45
"Rivington's Last Will..." 158
Robin, Claude 16, 54, 112
Ross, James 156
Rousseau 46, 118, 145
Royal Gazette 40
"Ruins of a Country-Church..." 57
"Rules and Directions..." 48
"Rules by Which a Great Empire..." 83
"Rules for changing a limited Republican Government..." 83

"Sailor's Relief" 47
St. James Island 30
Santa Cruz 15, 27, 30, 34
"Sciota Indian's Complaint" 63
Scorpion 36
Scott, Walter 171
"Scots, Wha Hae' " 167
Scull, William 36
"Sea-Voyage" 33
"Sentiments of a Republican" 82
"Serious Menace" 149
Sewell 130
"Shadrach and Pomposo" 140
Shakespeare, William 20, 175, 181
Shelley 121
"Short Canes!" 75
"Short Discourse upon Drunkenness" 60
"Short talk on Drunkenness" 103
"Sir Harry's Call" 29
"Sir Henry Clinton's Invitation to the Refugees" 29
"Sketch of... Vermont" 86
"Sketches of American History" 45, 158
"Sketches on Different Subjects" 116
Skirving 127
Spectator 24, 39, 41, 42, 59, 139, 145
Snyder, Simon 162
"Sorrowful petition of U, G, H..." 120
"Speech of a post..." 142
"Splenetic Indian" 46
Spy 37
"Stanzas as Written at Oratava ..." 154
"Stanzas as Written on the Hill of Neversink..." 64
"Stanzas, Occasioned by the Death of Dr. Franklin" 58
"Stanzas on South Carolina" 152
"Stanzas on the Decease of Thomas Paine..." 157
"Stanzas Published at the Procession..." 158, 160
"Stanzas to the Memory of Gen. Washington..." 134
"Stanzas Written at Baltimore ..." 53
"Stanzas Written at the Island of Madeira" 153
"Stanzas Written on a visit to a field..." 175
"Stanzas written, several years, since..." 113
Stuart (author) 80
"Suggestion" 86
Suwarrof 162
Swaine, John 11, 12, 16, 60, 93
Swift, Jonathan 20, 112, 181

Tatler 41, 42
Taylor, John 7, 99
Tempest 175
That Rascal Freneau 19
"Theatre" 83
Time Piece 12, 17, 112, 114, 118, 120, 125, 127, 128, 129, 131,
"The treaty unmasked" 108
Three Years Travels 145
"To a Caty-Did" 168
"To a Night-Fly" 149
"To a Persecuted Philosopher" 141
"To a Republican..." 140
"To an Angry Zealot" 141
"To Duncan Doolittle" 122
"To Harriot" 53
"To Lydia" 159
"To Matilda" 115
"To My Book" 141
"To Myrtalis" 147
"To Shylock Ap-Shenkin" 141
"To Sylvius on the Folly of Writing Poetry" 158
"To the Americans" 113
"To the Freemen of the United States" 88

"To the Frigate Constitution" 122
"To the National Gazette" 73
"To the Next Congress" 60
"To the Noblesse and Courtiers of the United States" 86
"To the Philadelphia Doctors" 122
"To the Squadrons on the Lakes" 166
"Tomb of the Patriots" 168
"Tomo Cheeki" 61, 63, 99, 101, 103, 104, 106, 108, 112, 142, 145, 162, 182
Travels of the Imagination 27
Travels Through North-America 16, 112
Travels Through North and South Carolina, Georgia, East and West Florida, 106, 145
True American 13, 19, 28, 153, 174, 179
"True American News Boys Annual Address" 174
Trumbull, John 63, 70
Tryon 28
Tucker, St. George 77

United States Magazine 6, 28, 30-34
"Upon a very Ancient Dutch House in Long-Island" 25
"Useful Animad versions" 82
"Useful, only in Vogue at Court" 140

Verplanck, Julian 179
"Verse to the Memory of Capt. Nicholas Biddle" 36
"Verses Made at Sea" 11, 38, 45
"Verses, on the arrival of the President..." 69
"View of Massachusetts" 57
"View of Rhode Island" 57
"Village Merchant" 71, 141
Virgil 20, 23, 181
"Virtue of Tobacco" 11
"Vision of the Night (A Fragment)" 32, 158
"Visions of Mirzah" 47
Voltaire 145
"Volunteer's March" 167, 181
Voyage to Boston 20
"Voyage of Timberoo-Tabo-Eede..." 49

Waln, Robert 179
War of 1812, 13
"War! War!! War!!! 111
"Warning to America" 141, 163
Warren 26, 43
Warton, A. 145
Washington, George 11, 17, 23, 26, 56, 58, 64, 73, 87, 89, 90, 99, 100, 108, 109, 112, 128, 134, 137, 143, 145, 147, 182
Webster, Noah 108, 119, 120, 124-6, 182
"Western Discoveries" 192
West Indies 15, 29
Wilcocks 111
"Wild Honey Suckle" 13, 32, 44, 52, 53, 64, 99, 101, 121, 153, 158, 169, 171, 181, 182
"Williams, S. T." 179
Witherspoon, John 15
"Winter" 177, 178
Wolcot, John 58
Wordsworth, William 145, 171, 181
"Written at Port Royal" 158

Yale 126